T0331945

Beyond Quick Fixes

Beyond Quick Fixes

Addressing the Complexity &
Uncertainties of Contemporary Society

William B. Rouse

OXFORD
UNIVERSITY PRESS

Great Clarendon Street, Oxford, OX2 6DP,
United Kingdom

Oxford University Press is a department of the University of Oxford.
It furthers the University's objective of excellence in research, scholarship,
and education by publishing worldwide. Oxford is a registered trade mark of
Oxford University Press in the UK and in certain other countries

Published in the United States of America by Oxford University Press
198 Madison Avenue, New York, NY 10016, United States of America

British Library Cataloguing in Publication Data
Data available

Library of Congress Control Number: 2023935127

ISBN 978-0-19-889253-3

DOI: 10.1093/oso/9780198892533.001.0001

Printed and bound by
CPI Group (UK) Ltd, Croydon, CR0 4YY

Preface

We often compare ourselves to the other thirty-six countries in the Organization for Economic Cooperation and Development (OECD). The US spends the most per capita on healthcare, but achieves much poorer outcomes than most OECD countries. The US is among the largest spenders on education in terms of costs per student. Yet, the US achieves far poorer educational outcomes than most OECD countries. How can we perform so poorly?

We tend to apply near-term "band aids" to these challenges, which inevitably are insufficient. We have adopted this approach for climate change and the fires, storms, floods, and so on that increasingly assault us, as well as to the impending rising sea levels. We spend mightily on disaster recovery, build everything back, and wait for disaster to strike again. We seem unable to adopt and fund longer-term approaches to improving the health, education, and energy fundamentals of our society.

There has to be a better way. In *Beyond Quick Fixes*, I step back from business as usual to rethink how we can approach the complex challenges of contemporary society. I retreat, initially, into the principles of design thinking rather than policymaking. My intent is to rigorously reconsider our typical modes of operation and explore alternative ways of thinking about complex problems and potential solutions. The result is an integrated approach to addressing complexity to assist leaders and advisors responsible for addressing these challenges.

This book is the result of a long journey addressing the challenges highlighted throughout this exposition. I have been involved in significant endeavors to "fix" various aspects of our ecosystems for health, education, and energy. We have made progress but this often seemed like a game of "whack a mole." Progress in particular areas often did not scale to progress in general.

This has all become much more complicated by the pervasive epidemic of misinformation and disinformation enabled by the technology of social media. Now, many people do not trust our understanding of best practices in health, education, and energy. Reaching a consensus on ways forward is much more challenging. Our approaches to the challenges of health, education, and energy now must include consideration of how to remediate misinformation and disinformation.

Beyond Quick Fixes is intended to support leaders and advisors responsible for addressing these challenges to gain a much deeper understanding of the behavioral, social, and economic phenomena that, if unaddressed, will likely undermine the progress of their initiatives. This understanding will not necessarily guarantee progress, but it will decrease the frequency of unfortunate surprises and provide insights into how best to adapt and avoid debilitating consequences.

The insights and approaches provided in this book are based on a wide range of lessons learned working with highly motivated and talented people focused on improving health, education, and energy processes and practices. Misinformation and disinformation have now made this much more complicated. Nevertheless, these people remain committed to making significant progress toward better processes and practices. It is remarkable to be able to work with them.

William B. Rouse
Washington, DC
February 2023

Contents

List of Figures

List of Tables

1
Chaos and Confusion

Four Societal Challenges That Seem Overwhelming

Introduction

We seem to be stuck, staring at insurmountable challenges. The pandemic is the opening act for climate change. We need to get much better at anticipating and preparing for these types of challenges. Simply rebuilding bridges once they fall, or houses once they are swept away, is both expensive and risks human lives. Anticipation and preparation costs more now, but is much less costly over time. Of course, spending now to save later is not a dominant American tradition.

We have managed—or at least reacted to—the AIDS epidemic (1981–2013), Internet bubble bursting (2001), the real estate bubble bursting (2007), the opioid epidemic (2017), forest fires on the West Coast (2018), and the coronavirus pandemic (2020). Very recently, we have experienced the fall of Afghanistan (2021), the latest earthquake and hurricane in Haiti (2021), and the attack on Ukraine (2022). Various earthquakes, hurricanes, and recently cicadas, but fortunately not locusts, have been sprinkled throughout.

Thus, we are increasingly encountering a mix of natural and human-made misfortunes. We spend enormous sums, usually after the fact, but achieve marginal outcomes. Too little, too late seems to be our slogan. We are trapped by our underperformance, feeling too busy to change. As Stephen Covey (1989) has characterized, we are often ensnared by the urgent but unimportant.

Beyond Quick Fixes. William B. Rouse, Oxford University Press. © William B. Rouse (2023).
DOI: 10.1093/oso/9780198892533.003.0001

We pursue quick fixes such as illustrated by the policy failures in Table 1.1. The result is unexpected negative consequences due to how key stakeholders react. These reactions were quite rational and could have been predicted with analysis of likely behavioral and social phenomena. US culture and politics also played a role. Policies

Table 1.1 Example Quick Fixes and Consequences

Domain	Quick Fix	Consequences	Interpretation
Health	Medicare imposed a 3% penalty on hospitals that readmitted patients within 30 days of the last admission for the same morbidity	Most hospitals preferred to accept penalties rather than lose revenue from readmitted patients, particularly hospitals with low bed occupancy rates (Rouse et al., 2019)	Did not consider the economics of the decision from key stakeholders' perspectives
Education	Federal government, via the No Child Left Behind Act of 2001, put test-based accountability into federal law, subsequently solidifying the state standardized test as the sole benchmark through which all schools were measured	As the annual progress of schools was judged by single standardized tests in reading and mathematics, the panic created by such a policy had a snowball effect of emphasizing passing the test over the general quality of the school experience: the more emphasis placed on test scores, the less emphasis placed on the general school experience (Schul, 2011)	Did not consider how mandate would change priorities of key stakeholders
Energy	Federal government (and some states) subsidized purchases of hybrid and battery-powered electric vehicles	Would-be buyers of highly fuel-efficient internal combustion vehicles accept subsidies, making it more difficult for automakers to meet US CAFÉ standards without cutting prices below costs, causing increased prices for large SUVs and pickup trucks (Liu, Rouse, & Hanawalt, 2018)	Did not consider how multiple federal priorities conflicted

that are not based on a broader understanding of the context within which deployment will occur face risks of these types of failures.

There has to be a better way. In this book, I step back from business as usual to rethink how we can approach the complex challenges of contemporary society. I retreat, initially, into the principles of design thinking rather than policymaking. My intent is to rigorously reconsider our typical modes of operation and explore alternative ways of thinking about complex problems and potential solutions. The result is an integrated approach to addressing complexity to assist the leaders and advisors responsible for addressing these challenges.

Societal Challenges

I consider challenges and uncertainties in terms of economic growth, health and education, energy and climate, and the roaring infodemic summarized in Table 1.2. I describe the problems that we have to address in these ecosystems, the sources of these problems, and how we tend to think about these problems and potential solutions. Understanding and deep thinking about the phenomena underlying these challenges are the central concerns.

The leaders charged with addressing these problems are stymied. Their efforts to "fix" these problems have involved decades of false starts for health, education, and energy, as well as seemingly overwhelming obstacles for mis/disinformation (e.g., laws relating to freedom of speech). Simply labeling something a "moon shot" is not the same as having a compelling vision and an executable plan. What is needed is not more meetings and discussions, but rather rethinking the overall approach to such challenges.

The four challenges are strongly affected by the designed fragmentation of the US political system, leading to fifty jurisdictions for licensing doctors, lawyers, and engineers, as well as 3,500 local public health agencies and 14,000 local school boards. "States' rights," as defined by the US Constitution, have driven this and undermined efforts to foster integrated solutions.

Table 1.2 Four Societal Challenges

Attributes	Challenges			
	Population Health	Lifelong Education	Energy and Climate	Mis/Disinformation
Overarching problem	Fragmented delivery system	Fragmented oversight system	Entrenched vested interests	Technology enabled infodemic
Overarching challenge	Vested interests in status quo	Philosophy of local control	Transitioning overall economy	Commitment to freedom of speech
Overarching solution	Information sharing and care coordination	Communicating and supporting national best practices	Renewable energy sources; solar, wind, hydro, nuclear	Societal immunity system that requires evidence
Implementation challenges	Competition against standardization	Pervasive "not invented here" mentality	Transitioning capital and creating jobs	Requires education from K-12 through college
Financing implementation	Moderate with downstream savings	Moderate but support needed for operating costs	Substantial if stranded assets subsidized	Modest but consistency needs maintenance
Sources of financing	Health providers and payers; federal incentives	Federal, state, and local education agencies	Corporate with federal incentives and subsidies	Free online offerings supported by philanthropy
Time frame for success	5–10 years due to current technology competencies	10–20 years due to 14,000 local school boards in US	10–20 years due to immense infrastructure changes	5–10 years to see immunity among children and adults

The effects of fragmentation are pervasive (e.g., Zegart, 2022). However, we have occasionally surmounted these obstacles:

- Social security is nationwide
- Medicare is nationwide
- Medicaid is state based but 50% federally funded
- Military services are nationwide
- DoD, DoE, NASA, NSF, and other research agendas are nationwide
- Many laws and regulations are nationwide

How can something that is fragmented become integrated and coordinated nationwide? I systematically address this question in this book, and suggest means to substantial progress on the four challenges, as well as in general. I hasten to note that this approach does **not** include literally integrating everything organizationally. Such nationalization is inconsistent with the culture of the US, and would involve the risks that Scott (1998) outlines.

There are strong interactions among these four ecosystems as shown in Figure 1.1. Educated people tend to be healthier. Inequalities in access to care often undermine health. Consequences of climate change will inordinately affect the uneducated and unhealthy.

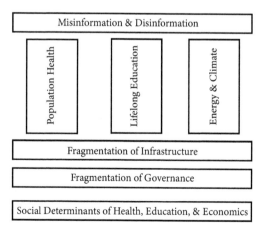

Figure 1.1 Context of Four Challenges

Misinformation and disinformation are pervasive, and exacerbate the other three challenges. The interactions among these phenomena are important, as a whack-a-mole approach to each challenge will be costly and unproductive. A more integrated approach is needed, an approach embodied by understanding and thought—more than slogans and pundits' proclamations.

Consider the interactions in Figure 1.1. Misinformation and disinformation pose enormous public health risks (Rouse, Johns, & Stead, 2022). Misleading advertisements (e.g., oxycontin) and misinformed or deceptive media pundits cause people to adopt practices to their detriment, or perhaps death. Such misinformation and disinformation are protected by free speech rights.

Education can provide the means to deter and mitigate misinformation and disinformation. It has been shown that students can learn how to detect, diagnose, and remediate false claims. There are compelling and viable proposals for how best to foster mental immunity to misinformation and disinformation (Norman, 2021). I later return to these possibilities.

People's orientation toward energy and climate, and associated behaviors, are strongly affected by misinformation and disinformation. Vested interests in the fossil-based energy industries, as well as politicians that depend on campaign contributions for these industries do their best to mislead the overall population (Yergin, 2020). As a result, people are skeptical of claims about the impact of carbon emissions on global warming.

Who is concerned with these issues—beyond everybody! My target audience includes both public and private sector leaders and advisors of endeavors to address these four challenge problems. This exposition provides a field guide to deep understanding of the problems being faced and how a broader design philosophy can enable transcending a "fix it" mentality to one of based on deep understanding, collaborative search for explanations and ways forward, and broad communication and involvement of key stakeholders.

My intention is to help these leaders and advisors to move beyond stuckness to the freedom and creativity of a powerful yet flexible design framework. This involves a philosophically coherent framework, but more importantly and helpfully, insights and guidance on how to best address these problems challenging society. Readers interested in these problems, or charged with addressing them, will find the practical guidance of great help.

Leaders charged with addressing these problems are highly frustrated. Enormous energies have been invested with little real progress. Pessimism in the four challenge domains is rampant. The time is right for cleaning the slate and populating plans with much that is familiar but integrated in innovative new ways.

Overview of book

Chapter 1, Chaos and Confusion, sets the stage for the overall book. The frustrations and overall lack of success in addressing societal challenges are outlined. The shortcomings of interventions intended to "fix" the problems are chronicled. The phenomena blocking progress are elaborated. It is argued that success depends on understanding the underlying causes of problems and developing means to remediate these causes.

I address challenges and uncertainties in terms of economic growth, health and education, energy and climate, and the roaring infodemic summarized in Table 1.2. I describe the problems that we have to address in these ecosystems, the sources of these problems, and how we tend to think about these problems and potential solutions. Understanding and deep thinking are the key elements.

As noted earlier, there are strong interactions among these four ecosystems. Educated people tend to be healthier. Inequalities in access to care often undermine health. The consequences of climate change will inordinately affect the uneducated and unhealthy. Misinformation and disinformation are pervasive. The interactions among these phenomena are important, as quick-fix approaches to each challenge will be costly and unproductive. A more integrated approach is needed, an approach embodied with understanding and thought.

Chapter 2, Broader Perspectives, explores the limitations of typical approaches to problem-solving. The underlying positivistic philosophy is elaborated. This philosophy is overwhelmingly solution rather than problem-driven. The idea is to quickly "fix" deficiencies rather than first deeply explore the reasons for the deficiencies.

The complexity of the four challenges has some technological elements, but is driven by behavioral, social, and political phenomena. This chapter explores historical and contemporary findings in economics, psychology, social psychology, sociology, and politics. Behavioral and social phenomena underlie the challenges in Table 1.2, both as sources of dysfunctional designs and impediments to creative, sustainable change. Understanding these phenomena is necessary to inform how we address remediating the challenges.

I present a design-oriented approach that is elaborated in terms of wicked problems, complex adaptive systems, and human-centered design, a process of considering and balancing the value, concerns, and perceptions of key stakeholders in any endeavor. Stakeholders, attributes, and preferences are central constructs.

Chapter 3, Insights for Addressing Challenges, addresses engaging reality as it is rather than what you assumed or hoped it would be. The fundamental question concerns what evidence-based knowledge is available for understanding the physical, behavioral, and social phenomena underlying the challenges at hand. Addressing this question requires conducting rigorous evidence-based analysis of underlying phenomena and alternative courses of action.

Table 1.3 illustrates the range of topics addressed in this chapter. Succinctly, the focus is on the phenomena underlying the four societal challenges. This both illustrates the thinking required and provides a basis for continuing the pursuit of these challenges.

A fundamental question concerns where change interventions should be targeted. Several questions should guide these choices:

- Will the benefits envisioned be embraced by stakeholders?
- Is any stakeholder organization currently providing these benefits?
- Are they successfully providing these benefits?

Table 1.3 Insights into Challenges

Attributes	Challenges			
	Population Health	Lifelong Education	Energy and Climate	Mis/Disinformation
Underlying physical, behavioral and social phenomena	Disease, prevention, treatment	Learning, practicing, experiencing, collaborating	Emissions of carbon, methane, and so on	Rumoring, deception, manipulation, trust
Delivery of associated goods and services	Providers, payers, suppliers (e.g., drugs and devices)	Schools, colleges, publishers	Extraction, conversion, transmission, distribution, consumption	Social media, broadcast media, Internet more broadly
Effectiveness of delivery ecosystem	Inadequate information sharing and care coordination; misaligned incentives	Inadequate communication and support of educational best practices	Inadequate renewable energy sources; solar, wind, hydro, nuclear; infrastructure	Inadequate societal immunity system that requires evidence to support beliefs
Beneficiaries of delivery ecosystem	Patients, 16 million employees, companies, shareholders	Students, 15 million employees, companies, shareholders	Everyone, 7 million employees, companies, shareholders	Advertisers, politicians, pundits
Societal values and norms	Health as a public vs. private good	Education as a public vs. private good	Freedom of choice	Freedom of speech

- Is the scope of those benefited limited by resources or mandates?
- What might hinder the broad provision of these benefits?

There are many entrenched rice bowls in healthcare in terms of providers, payers, pharma, and so on. However, Social Security provided a highly valued benefit in 1935 and did not disrupt existing rice bowls. My sense is that mental health, as a broadly defined public health challenge, is not as sclerotic. Consequently, nationwide federal investment in standards, guidelines, and treatment might be welcomed.

In education, nationwide federal investments in STEM (science, technology, engineering, and math) and STW (skilled technical workforce) in terms of standards, guidelines, and curricula might be welcomed, particularly in communities challenged to perform. In energy, nationwide federal investments in renewables, Generation 3 nuclear, storage, and transmission are already major commitments; workforce retraining not so much. In mis/disinformation, nationwide federal policies will predominate. Education on information management and mental immunity initiatives will be locally delivered.

This discussion includes a diagram of how these initiatives influence each other, both negatively and positively. For example, health and education interact to undermine or reinforce each other. Misinformation and disinformation undermine health, can be mitigated by education, and confuse stakeholders with regard to energy initiatives.

Chapter 4, Translating Insights into Action Plans, involves transforming the findings in Table 1.2 into alternative course of action, as well as explaining findings and alternative courses of action in stakeholder-friendly formats. Acting in transparent ways that stakeholders can understand and evaluate is central to stakeholders trusting change.

My approach to assessing alternative actions is distinctly model based (Rouse, 2015; Rouse et al., 2019) in terms of employing computational models to project possible consequences of alternative

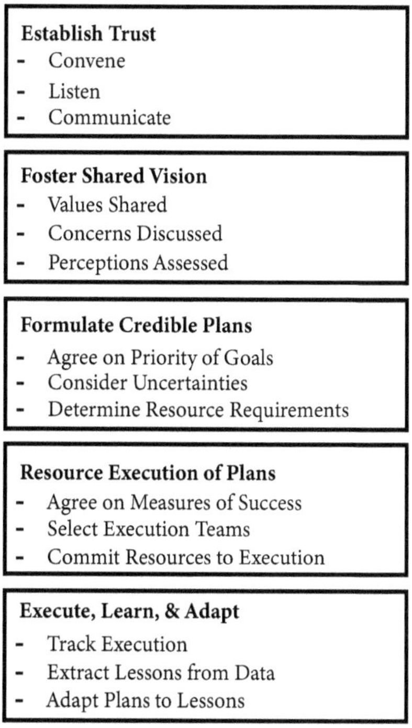

Establish Trust
- Convene
- Listen
- Communicate

Foster Shared Vision
- Values Shared
- Concerns Discussed
- Perceptions Assessed

Formulate Credible Plans
- Agree on Priority of Goals
- Consider Uncertainties
- Determine Resource Requirements

Resource Execution of Plans
- Agree on Measures of Success
- Select Execution Teams
- Commit Resources to Execution

Execute, Learn, & Adapt
- Track Execution
- Extract Lessons from Data
- Adapt Plans to Lessons

Figure 1.2 Gaining and Sustaining Stakeholder Support

interventions in health, education, energy, and mis/disinformation. Such representations are often important to leveraging investments across challenges.

Table 1.4 illustrates how understanding translates into multi-stage courses of action. This chapter discusses these potential aspirational courses of action in considerable detail, including how stakeholders will be supported to understand and trust these alternative ways forward for each challenge. The process for gaining and sustaining stakeholder support is shown in Figure 1.2.

Why should we believe that the aspirations elaborated in Table 1.4 are achievable? Are there any examples of success in pursuing such multi-stage plans? What can we learn from these examples?

In every domain, there are people or organizations whose uncommon behaviors and strategies enable them to formulate and implement better solutions to problems than their peers, while having

Table 1.4 Insights into Actions

Aspirations	Challenges			
	Population Health	Lifelong Education	Energy and Climate	Mis/Disinformation
Starting point (status quo)	High costs and poor outcomes	High costs and poor outcomes	Unacceptable emission levels	Chaos and confusion
Baseline initial success	Information sharing	National graduation standards	Emission limitations	Social media limitations
Leveraging baseline	Care coordination across services	National curriculum standards for STEM and STW	Renewables, including nuclear	Free speech with responsibility
Innovative leaps	Single payer	Elimination of reliance on property taxes	Storage and transmission innovations	Education on information management
Ultimate success	Integrated delivery system	Integrated delivery system	Green energy workforce	Pervasive mental immunity

access to the same resources and facing similar or worse challenges. Such people or organizations are termed **positive deviants**.

I discuss compelling examples for each of the four challenges in this chapter. We have experienced success in pursuing aspirations such as those summarized in Table 1.4. It is quite useful to learn why and how these successes resulted.

Chapter 5, Integrating Plans into Solutions, addresses how integrated solutions will create beneficial outcomes for all stakeholders and not undermine others. Table 1.5 illustrates several overall components of benefits to stakeholders.

This chapter is primarily concerned with how all the pieces fit together. There are not four disparate challenges—they all fit and play together. Beyond common objectives and functional needs, they can be enhanced by intelligent systems technology. Human-centered support is both imaginable and feasible.

I address this integration as a human-centered design problem. Stakeholders' attributes and preferences are addressed at multiple levels. At the highest level, stakeholders are concerned with health and education outcomes, energy availability, and trusted information sources. At a lower level, stakeholders are more focused on the information infrastructure that enables these outcomes.

The design of this infrastructure can be greatly enhanced by the appropriate use of intelligent systems technology. I elaborate on the functional needs this technology can provide. Two use case scenarios are provided, one involving driverless cars for people with disabilities, and the other focused on cognitive assistance for clinicians. I discuss the ways in which these two scenarios address the four challenges.

Chapter 6, Economic Modeling of Investment Impacts, focuses on the economic realities of pursuing the functionality elaborated in Chapter 5. There will be revenue generated and costs saved over decades. The accounting for these cash flows needs to cross agencies and, of course, years. We are concerned not only with next year's budget, but next decade's society.

Economic integration is a key to affordable change. The economic model that I present considers the investments and returns

Table 1.5 Actions and Consequences

Attributes	Challenges			
	Population Health	Lifelong Education	Energy and Climate	Mis/Dis Information
Understanding and benefiting all stakeholders	Patients, families, clinicians, providers, payers	Students, parents, teachers, employers	Consumers, providers, employees	Communicators, consumers, overseers
Transcending current perceptions and experiences	Clarifying and amending hidden assumptions	Clarifying and amending hidden assumptions	Clarifying and amending hidden assumptions	Clarifying and amending hidden assumptions
Fostering ultimate awareness of benefits	Communicating value and pursuit of health	Communicating value and pursuit of education	Communicating value and pursuit of conservation	Communicating value and pursuit of vetted info
Broadly sharing insights with stakeholders	Broadcasting success story to broad audience	Broadcasting success story to broad audience	Broadcasting success story to broad audience	Broadcasting success story to broad audience
Learning that fosters addressing the next challenge	Integrating lessons learned about health	Integrating lessons learned about education	Integrating lessons learned on conservation	Integrating mental immunity lessons learned

associated with addressing the challenges in an integrated manner. The concern is with money flows over decades. The overarching focus is on money flows across government entities—IRS, SSA, CMS, and others. For example:

- HHS invests money
- DOE (education) invests money
- DOE (energy) invests money
- IRS collects money
- SSA provides money
- CMS reimburses money

These siloes will undoubtedly push back against changes. However, this chapter projects the value to the whole country, not just for particular agencies. I consider the baselines:

- Continued fragmented fee for services healthcare vs. population health
- Continued fragmented education vs. integrated high-quality lifelong education
- Continued reliance on fossil fuels vs. transitioning to renewable energy sources
- Continued mis/dis infodemic vs. educated and mentally immune population

Evidence-based quantitative projections are used to illustrate the economic benefits of the solutions articulated in Chapter 5.

Chapter 7, Scaling Solutions for Broad Benefits, concerns the need to continually motivate and resource ongoing change. This includes understanding and balancing economics across siloes and ecosystems. The overarching goal is to circumvent the "valley of death" whereby successful pilot tests are not scaled and sustained. Beyond proving that a particular intervention will help a small, targeted population, sustained motivation and resources are needed to benefit everybody. Successful execution is central to transforming inventive ideas into societal innovations, and indeed social movements.

Chapter 8, Overcoming Common Hurdles, focuses on organizational and individual change. Learning and growth are central but require reflection and absorption. This has to be pursued while responding to natural and human-made challenges, including:

- When the competition surprises you
- When we misunderstand the signals
- When no one owns the problem
- When the unpopular position is correct
- When secondary issues dominate
- When the organization is in the way
- When personalities trump competence
- When abilities to execute are secondary
- When stakeholders thwart change
- When leadership makes a difference

This chapter concludes with practical guidance on how to sense, understand, and respond to such obstacles.

Epilogue

What if my evidence, courses of action, and communications in this book are not convincing? Joseph Tainter's ***The Collapse of Complex Societies*** (1988) presaged Jared Diamond's ***Collapse: How Societies Choose to Fail or Succeed*** (2004). Both books provide vivid explanations of how societies fail and why.

Societies create mechanisms to deal with new challenges. Walls are built to thwart Mongol hoards. Regulations are created to deter fraud and corruption. Programs are designed to assure equity of access to education and health. Each of these initiatives leads to a new layer of societal complexity.

Each of these layers creates a set of vested interests in the operations of the layer and the economic benefits of these operations.

Consequently, it is very difficult to eliminate layers, even if the original motivation for the layer has disappeared.

Adding layers is much easier. The benefits of the layer, to both those targeted to receive these benefits and those compensated to provide these benefits, can be quite substantial. That's why they are very reluctant to forego these benefits, even if the provision of these benefits no longer makes sense.

So, societies keep adding layers that consume resources. Eventually, a new challenge emerges—a pandemic, climate change, or alien invaders—and there are no resources to invest in a new layer. All resources are being consumed to support earlier layers of complexity. This is a harbinger of societal failure. This book is intended to help us avoid this fate.

References

Covey, S.R. (1989). *The 7 Habits of Highly Effective People.* New York: Free Press.

Diamond, J. (2004) *Collapse: How Societies Choose to Fail or Succeed* New York: Viking Press.

Liu, C., Rouse, W.B., & Hanawalt, E. (2018). Adoption of powertrain technologies in automobiles: A system dynamics model of technology diffusion in the American market. *IEEE Transactions on Vehicular Technology,* 67 (7), 5621–5634.

Norman, A. (2021). *Mental Immunity: Infectious Ideas, Mind-Parasites, and the Search for a Better Way to Think.* New York: Harper.

Rouse, W.B. (2015). *Modeling and Visualization of Complex Systems and Enterprises: Explorations of Physical, Human, Economic, and Social Phenomena.* New York: Wiley.

Rouse, W.B. (2019). *Computing Possible Futures: Model-Based Explorations of "What if?"* Oxford, UK: Oxford University Press.

Rouse, W.B, Johns, M.M.E., & Stead, W.W. (2022). *Medical Misinformation & Disinformation.* Washington, DC: McCourt School of Public Policy, Georgetown University.

Rouse, W.B., Naylor, M.D., Yu, Z., Pennock, M.P., Hirschman, K.B., Pauly, M.V., & Pepe, K.P. (2019). Policy flight simulators: Accelerating decisions to adopt evidence-based health interventions. *Journal of Healthcare Management*, 64 (4), 231–241.

Schul, J.E. (2011). *Unintended Consequences: Fundamental Flaws That Plague the No Child Left Behind Act*. Ada, OH: Ohio Northern University.

Scott, J.C. (1998). *Seeing Like a State: How Certain Schemes to Improve the Human Condition Have Failed*. New Haven, CT: Yale University Press.

Tainter, J. (1988). *The Collapse of Complex Societies*. Cambridge, UK: Cambridge University Press.

Yergin, D. (2020). *The New Map: Energy, Climate, and the Clash of Nations*. New York: Penguin Press.

Zegart, A.B. (2022). *Spies, Lies & Algorithms: The History and Future of American Intelligence*. Princeton, NJ: Princeton University Press.

2

Broader Perspectives

Addressing Underlying Behavioral and Social Phenomena

A bit over two decades ago, I published the best-selling ***Don't Jump to Solutions*** (Jossey-Bass, 1998), with the subtitle ***Thirteen Delusions That Undermine Strategic Thinking***. It was selected as the Doubleday Book of the Month, and was named one of the top twenty management books published globally that year. I discussed numerous case studies of how well-known enterprises quickly moved to developing solutions before they fully understood the problems they were facing.

Much more recently, I published ***Modeling and Visualization of Complex Systems and Enterprises*** (Rouse, 2015), with the subtitle ***Explorations of Physical, Human, Economic, and Social Phenomena***. This book addresses engineers' strong inclinations to jump to solutions before they fully understood the problems being pursued. A major theme of this book was the need to explore the phenomena underlying problems before formulating solutions.

This chapter explores the limitations of typical approaches to problem-solving when facing the types of challenges introduced in the past chapter. The typical problem-solving philosophy is overwhelmingly solution-oriented rather than problem-driven. The idea is to quickly "fix" deficiencies rather than first deeply explore the reasons for the deficiencies. Consequently, fixes are only temporary, at best.

Why is population health so difficult to achieve? Why is lifelong education so seldom accomplished? Why do people misunderstand the risks and consequences associated with energy and climate? Why

Beyond Quick Fixes. William B. Rouse, Oxford University Press. © William B. Rouse (2023). DOI: 10.1093/oso/9780198892533.003.0002

does society tolerate the infodemic of misinformation and disinformation? If we cannot answer these questions, why do we think we can solve these problems?

I address the answers to these questions more fully in the next chapter. However, it is useful to provide thumbnail sketches of the answers here. Behavioral and social phenomena underlie the challenges in Table 1.2, both as sources of dysfunctional designs and impediments to creative, sustainable change. The layers of Figure 1.1 emphasize the endemic nature of these impediments.

Findings from Behavioral and Social Sciences

Pervasive behavioral and social phenomena underlie the four challenges. Technically oriented "fixes" that do not account for these phenomena are likely to quickly fail to achieve the ends sought. I will start with economics, which Paul Samuelson argued is the queen of social sciences. I will not, however, address this controversial perspective.

Economics

There are two long-standing debates in economics that fundamentally affect how one views the four challenges and how they can best be addressed. The two sides of the first debate are often associated with Friedrich Hayek and Milton Friedman on one side and John Maynard Keynes and Karl Polanyi on the other. Wapshott (2011) and Delong (2022) elaborate on this debate in considerable detail.

Succinctly, is economic growth driven by market forces or government planning? Hayek and Friedman argue that market forces determine everything and government should stay out of the way. Keynes and Polanyi counter that market forces are important, but can sometimes result in disruptive outcomes, like discrimination and unemployment, that markets are unwilling to address. The government needs to stabilize situations such as the Great Depression (1929–1939) and Great Recession (2007–2009).

Those touting the market economy argue that governments are terrible at picking winners and should let the marketplace enable winners to emerge through competitive forces. This does not always work, as demonstrated by the recently experienced real estate bubble (Lewis, 2011; Blinder, 2013).

In real estate mortgage markets, impenetrable derivative securities were bought and sold. The valuations and ratings of these securities were premised on any single mortgage default being a random event. In other words, the default of any particular mortgage was assumed to have no impact on the possible default of any other mortgage.

The growing demand for these securities pressurized mortgage companies to lower the standards for these loans. Easily available mortgages drove the sales of homes, steadily increasing home prices. Loans with initial periods of low, or even zero, interest attracted home buyers to adjustable-rate mortgages. Many of these people could not possibly make the mortgage payments when the rates were adjusted after the initial period.

This was of less concern than one might think because people expected to flip these houses by selling them quickly at significantly increased prices. This worked as long as prices continued increasing, but as more and more lower-quality mortgages were sold, the number of defaults increased and dampened the increasing prices, which led to further increases in defaults. The bubble quickly burst.

The defaults were not random events as assumed by those valuing these securities. They constituted what is termed a "common mode failure," where a common cause results in widespread failure. Thus, these securities were much more risky than sellers had advertised. The consequences of such misinformation were enormous.

Hayek would argue that risk-takers should earn rewards, but investment banks were not taking risks; they were selling risks that neither they nor the buyers understood. When the bubble burst, the banks and investment companies were bailed out by the government, with banks using some of this money to provide executive bonuses. Millions of homeowners lost their homes when they could not make increasing mortgage payments on homes that were now worth less than the mortgage.

The greed of investment companies and consumers buying houses they could not afford, because they intended to flip them, drove the bubble. Many understood what was happening and sold short these toxic assets. Michael Lewis, in **The Big Short,** notes that many of the smartest people were betting against the country. The market economy undermined the economy.

The implications for addressing the four challenges are quite clear. Profit seekers are often quite willing to manipulate the rules of the game to satisfy their greedy aspirations. Changes to the health, education, and energy ecosystems will threaten profits. Limits on misinformation and disinformation will affect both profits and votes. I do not think that the marketplace will simply support and adapt to such changes. Government will have to play a central role, perhaps facilitating rather than regulating, but nevertheless being active.

The second debate concerns sources of innovation and economic growth. Mokyr (1992) argues and illustrates how technology has long been the driver. There seems to be an emerging consensus that the US leadership in innovation has waned. Gordon (2016) has argued that 1870–1970 was the United States' century of innovation. I made the same argument, based on the same line of reasoning, a couple of years earlier (Rouse, 2014a).

More recently, DeLong (2022) proposed 1870–2007 as the country's "long century" of innovation, ending with the onset of the Great Recession. The rationale for 1970 as the end point is that social networking is not as compelling as electricity and indoor plumbing. Which one would you be willing to give up? On the other hand, social media has been a compelling source of disruption.

The relevance of this debate concerns the extent to which technologies will mitigate the challenges. My sense is that many existing technologies, if appropriately deployed and supported, can be leveraged to address the challenges. The hurdles are much more organizational and social than technological. Overcoming these hurdles involves thoughtful planning, execution, and learning, as discussed in Chapters 4 and 5.

Psychology

The economic landscape provides two tensions we need to address. Unfortunately, these tensions are complicated by the psychological orientations of the people in these ecosystems. First of all, typical economists' assumptions do not reflect reality. When Andy Sage and I were writing a new edition of his economics textbook (Sage & Rouse, 2011), I observed that the assumptions that markets know everything and stakeholders maximize expected utility were very unrealistic. He responded that without these assumptions, he could not solve the equations.

I undertook a study of the economic value of investing in people (Rouse, 2010). The concern was with the valuation of investments in people's training and education, safety and health, and work productivity. It is usually possible to determine a positive return on such investments, with one major caveat. If the organization investing is the same organization that gets the returns, then investments usually happen. However, if the returns accrue to another organization, the investing organization sees the outlay as a cost and tries to minimize it.

For example, investing in technologies for people with disabilities to work or for elderly people to age at home can result in substantial savings for Medicare, Medicaid, and Social Security, but those monies do not flow to the National Institutes of Health, for example, to fund further investments. This disincentivizes decisions to increase the budget for such investments. I return to this phenomenon in Chapter 6.

Human decision-making is not always so crisply rational. Humans tend to be flawed decision-makers. Herbert Simon (1957, 1969, 1972) pioneered studies of bounded rationality and satisficing by humans (i.e., pursuing satisfactory rather than optimal decisions). George Miller's most famous discovery was that human short-term memory is generally limited to holding seven pieces of information, plus or minus two (Miller, 1956).

Ward Edwards (1967) found that people have difficulty processing probabilistic information. Daniel Kahneman and Amos Tversky explored the heuristics and biases that limit effective decision-making (Kahneman, 2011). Biases include confirmation bias (only taking into account information that supports presuppositions), optimism bias (overestimating the likelihood of success), availability bias (overestimating the frequency of familiar events), and fundamental attribution error (inferring incorrect causation).

Henry Mintzberg (1975) researched the folklore of management decision-making and found that the belief that managers are reflective, careful optimizers is unfounded. Instead, typical managers are interrupt driven, spending a few minutes on each task. Gary Klein (2004) found that when professionals are faced with decisions they have addressed many times, their intuitions are often correct unless, of course, their perceptions that this is a familiar situation are unwarranted.

Kahneman and Richard Thaler have been pioneers in the field known as behavioral economics. Thaler's study of nudges (2009, 2015) has illustrated the subtlety of what may affect decisions. This integration of psychology into economic models is central to addressing the four challenges in this book. It makes no sense to assume that people will behave in ways that are unlikely, or perhaps impossible.

Training and aiding human decision-making can make a huge difference (Rouse, 2019). Training increases people's potential to perform. Aiding directly augments human performance. Thus, we can compensate for humans' limitations by enhancing abilities, overcoming limitations, and fostering acceptance of such assistance.

Social Psychology

We understand individual performance pretty well, as well as team performance. Social interactions and behaviors are much more complicated, especially for large social networks, which social media has enormously enlarged. We need to understand how to influence these networks if we are to successfully address the challenges of interest in this book.

Social psychology considers people and organizations in relation to each other. There are several aspects of social psychology that are particularly relevant to the challenges of interest in this book. A central issue is the extent to which people trust the information and guidance provided from various sources.

Klein (2020) explores polarization and identity politics. An increasing trend is for people to support candidates with whom they identify, regardless of their behaviors and policies. One dichotomy of importance is highly educated urban upper-middle-class people versus much less-educated rural working-class people. In a nutshell, blue-state versus red-state citizens. These two populations increasingly distrust each other.

Leonhardt (2022) argues that a crisis to democracy is coming, due to Republican refusal to accept election defeat and an increasing number of states' election officials continuing to embrace this perspective. Further, due to the electoral college and gerrymandering, government policy is becoming increasingly disconnected from public opinion. Policy decisions can win Congressional votes attributable to only a minority of citizen voters.

An interesting trait that differs between these two groups concerns "luxury beliefs." Edsall (2022) provides a review of studies on the phenomena of increasing education and income being associated with greater beliefs in fairness, equality, and opportunities for everyone. Higher-income people are willing to be taxed to pursue these ends. Lower-income people are much less supportive. This altruistic tendency does have limits. Marble and Nall (2021) report that liberal homeowners tend to be opposed to low-income housing being built next to their homes.

Many people's perceptions and beliefs are enormously affected by social media (e.g., Facebook and Twitter). Jonathan Haidt, a social psychologist, has explored the "dark" psychology of social networks (2019, 2022). He notes that "human beings evolved to gossip, preen, manipulate, and ostracize."

He argues that social capital, strong institutions, and shared stories collectively bind together successful democracies. Social media has weakened all three. Democracy depends on the widely internalized acceptance of the legitimacy of rules, norms, and institutions, but trust has seriously eroded this acceptance.

The impacts have tended to be pervasive. Social media does not make most people more aggressive, but enables a minority to troll the majority. "Social media deputizes everyone to administer justice with no due process." Most people become very reluctant to express any opinions.

Todd Rose (2022) explores the phenomena of collective illusions. He argues, "Social media platforms allow anyone who's got an axe to grind to pull a digital power play, exerting direct control over the perceived majority and scaring all dissenters into silence with their unfiltered vehemence." He concludes, "Compromising your personal integrity for the sake of belonging quietly wears away at your self-esteem and has been shown to negatively affect personal health in both the short and the long term."

He then observes:

> It's one thing to hide your true feelings about the dry turkey. It's another to obscure the truth around big social, moral, economic, or political issues. If someone makes a racist remark while passing the gravy, and nobody objects to it, the statement might appear acceptable when it obviously isn't. And when we're dealing with crucial social issues that extend far beyond the end of a fork, this reluctance to be open and authentic can cause serious, macro-level problems. Rose (2022)

Andy Norman (2021) asserts that we need to develop mental immunity to social media. He argues for collaborative inquiry as a means to address and mitigate misinformation and disinformation. There is some evidence that this has worked with school children. I return to Haidt, Rose, and Norman in later chapters.

Medical misinformation and disinformation provides a strong example of the impacts of social media, and the media in general, on public health (Rouse, Johns, & Stead, 2022). Television advertising convinces people to pay for and consume interventions that will not benefit them and may harm them. Many thousands of websites provide health advice for which there is no evidence of efficacy. Yet many people, desperate for help, follow this advice that, at best, is useless. I will explore this phenomenon in more detail in Chapter 3.

At an extreme, social media has been weaponized (Singer & Brooking, 2018; Zegart, 2022). Foreign adversaries undermine the trust of citizens in government and each other, even interfering with elections. Domestic political competitors spread misinformation and disinformation to persuade voters to support them, often with no intent to follow through on what they have promised. People then "like" and "retweet," and the false information gains increasing credibility.

Sociology

The approach I have adopted in this book characterizes public–private domains as complex networks of stakeholders and relationships that need to be understood and then incentivized and motivated to engage in fundamental change. Sociology offers other approaches to characterizing these ecosystems.

Sociology attempts to explain societal changes over time, often long times. A good example is the transition from agrarian to manufacturing to service economies. More specifically, this discipline focuses on explaining how we arrived at a current social situation (e.g., welfare state). They seldom address trying to predict the efficacy of near-term interventions.

Polanyi's classic book (1944) deals with transformation in terms of the social and political upheavals associated with the rise of the market economy. He argues that this has resulted in humanity's economic mentality changing. Prior to this transformation, people based their economies on reciprocity and redistribution across personal and communal relationships. Industrialization and increasing state influence led to competitive markets that undermined these previous social tendencies, replacing them with formal institutions that aimed to promote a self-regulating market economy.

This encouraged the myth of humans' propensity toward rational free trade. However, he asserts instead that "man's economy, as a rule, is submerged in his social relationships." He proposes an alternative ethnographic economic approach called "substantivism," in opposition to "formalism"—he coined both terms. He argues that markets cannot solely be understood through economic theory, as they are embedded in social and political logics, which makes it necessary to take into account politics.

Polanyi argues that the term *economics* has two meanings: the formal meaning refers to economics as the logic of rational action and decision-making, as a rational choice between the alternative uses of limited means. The second, substantive meaning, however, presupposes neither rational decision-making nor conditions of scarcity. It simply refers to the study of how humans make a living from their social and natural environment, which may or may not involve utility maximization. Anthropologists have embraced the substantive position as it does not impose western cultural assumptions on other societies.

Giddens (1979) provides a broad view both historically and culturally. He argues that there is a duality of structure by which social practice, his principal unit of investigation, has both a structural and an agency component. The structural environment constrains individual behavior, but it also makes it possible. Social actors are reflexive and monitor the ongoing flow of activities and structural conditions to adapt their actions to their evolving understandings.

Giddens calls this two-tiered, interpretive, and dialectical relationship between social scientific knowledge and human practices the double hermeneutic. He also stresses the importance of power, which provides means to ends, and hence is directly involved in the actions of every person. He emphasizes the transformative capacity of people to change the social and material world.

Habermas (1988) addresses legitimation and communication in his studies of the origins, nature, and evolution of public opinion in democratic societies. Feudal societies were transformed into bourgeois liberal constitutional entities that distinguished between the public and private realms, including a public sphere for rational-critical political debate leading to a new phenomenon called public opinion. Spearheading this shift was the growth of a literary public sphere in which the bourgeoisie learned to critically reflect upon itself and its role in society.

Habermas then traces the transition from the liberal bourgeois public sphere to the modern mass society of the social welfare state. The result was the rise of mass societies characterized by consumer capitalism in the twentieth century. The scope of Habermas' approach to transformation considers society over centuries. This book is not so ambitious in that the focus is on particular challenges (e.g., health and education), rather than all of society. Further, the time frame is decades at most, rather than centuries.

Luhmann (1995) focuses on a general theory of systems, with an emphasis on understanding meaning and communication. He is interested in cybernetic models that no longer require the assumption of the external observer. The cybernetic view of people, organizations, and society as composed of various levels of feedback control systems is consistent with the approach elaborated and applied in this book.

Castells (1996) provides a contemporary view of technology-mediated society. Based on research across many global regions, a systematic theory of the information society is formulated which reflects the fundamental effects of information technology on the contemporary world. He argues that "A network society is a society where the key social structures and activities are organized around electronically processed information networks."

This brief summary provides a perspective on how sociology addresses social systems. The goal is to explain social trends and events, often over long periods of time. This is very interesting, but the approach in this book needs to go further. Beyond explanation, we need to predict what stakeholders are likely to do, influence their choices and behaviors, and design interventions and incentives for their engagement in change.

The focus in this book is primarily on policy—either government policy or private sector management policy. To successfully pursue this goal, we need to understand the politics associated with the challenges of interest. This, in turn, requires that we understand stakeholders and their values, concerns, and perceptions.

Political Systems

The nature of a political system can both hinder and enable change. It is important to understand how a particular political system came to be and the implications for values, norms, structure, and rules.

Monarchies and autocracies long preceded democracies, although Athens had a limited democracy. Autocracies are usually led by a single supreme decision-maker, who often rules by force. Monarchies can be absolute or constitutional. The United Kingdom, Sweden, and Japan are good examples of the latter, where the monarch exercises their authority in accordance with a constitution and is not the sole decision-maker.

There is an important distinction between presidential and parliamentary democracies. In the presidential system of government, the leader is elected separately from the legislature. In the parliamentary system of government, the leader is a member of parliament. In presidential systems, people vote for particular candidates, while in parliamentary systems, people vote for parties, of which there are usually several.

A republic is a form of government in which the people hold power, but elect representatives to exercise that power. A republic is a federation when there is both a national government and governments of member states. A constitution usually defines the powers of the federal versus state governments.

In the US, at least, federation has resulted in fragmentation of services, across states, agencies, and companies. For example, the licensing of doctors, lawyers, and engineers differs across states, and these professionals can only practice in states where they are licensed and, of course, have passed various exams and paid the licensing fees.

The economics of such "siloes" undermine incentives for cross-cutting investments. These rice bowls defend the status quo and legacy commitments, thwarting moving resources to enable improvements. Information sharing and service coordination are hindered to protect siloes. Thus, there is no "system" in the US for healthcare delivery or education, for example.

This fragmentation is also rampant at the federal level. Congress creates rice bowls to benefit various constituencies. Coordination across these various commitments is quite poor, often non-existent. Khanna (2022) provides a compelling vision of how the US government could function much more effectively, benefiting everybody, not just those first in line.

The judicial system strongly impacts what can and cannot be accomplished. There are many aspects of this. The challenge of misinformation and disinformation is most affected by the First Amendment of the US Constitution, which protects freedom of speech. This strongly limits what the government can do to limit and mitigate misinformation and disinformation. Rosenberg (2021) chronicles the history of the First Amendment. I return to this topic in later chapters.

Summary

So, the behavioral, social, and political world is much more complicated than classical economics was—or is—prepared to address. Hence, the predictions of classical economists—at least, the academics—should be considered with caution. Their first priorities are equations that are solvable and theorems that are provable, thereby enabling promotions, tenure, and occasionally a Nobel Prize.

In the remainder of this chapter, I outline an approach elaborated in terms of wicked problems, complex adaptive systems, and human-centered design. This approach enables gaining a deep understanding of the challenges being addressed, including the behavioral and social phenomena that will strongly affect the likely success of addressing the four challenges.

Wicked Problems

The four challenges easily qualify as "wicked problems." Horst Rittel, almost five decades ago, characterized addressing such challenges as wicked problems. A wicked problem is a social or cultural problem laced with incomplete or contradictory knowledge, large numbers of people and opinions involved, substantial economic burdens, and the interconnected nature of these problems with other problems. Problems such as poverty, sustainability, equality, health and wellness, and climate change challenge our nation and our world.

Consider Rittel's ten characteristics of wicked problems (Rittel & Webber, 1973). Wicked problems have no definitive formulation (i.e., they are not exemplars of any standard taxonomy of problems). It is difficult to measure or claim success in solving wicked problems, in part because solutions can be only better or worse, but not correct or incorrect.

Given the uniqueness of each wicked problem, there are no best practices that can be adopted from previous problem-solving. This is due, in part, to every problem being a symptom of other problems. This is aggravated by there always being multiple explanations for problems, especially when there are many stakeholders.

Solutions to problems involve single chances of success because one is trying to address a moving target driven by the complex adaptive nature of the ecosystem. Consequently, solution strategies have no definitive validity tests. Dealing with such situations requires that policy decision-makers be empowered and responsible, keeping in mind that rarely is there one decision authority.

Table 2.1 summarizes how these ten characteristics are manifested across our four challenges. I elaborate on each of these assessments in Chapter 3.

Overall Approach to Wicked Problems

In this section, I provide several qualitative guidelines for approaching fundamental change in complex adaptive organizational ecosystems. In subsequent sections, I will discuss the quantitative analytic framework for addressing the details of pursuing such changes.

Table 2.1 Attributes of Wicked Problems across Four Challenges

Wicked Problem Attributes	Relevance to Challenges
No definitive problem formulation	Symptoms not uniquely attributable to problems
Difficult to measure success	Difficult to attribute consequences to interventions
Solutions not correct or incorrect	Cannot "solve" the challenges
No solution best practices	Hindered by lack of repeated experiences
Multiple problem explanations	Stakeholders have varying explanations
Multiple interrelated problems	Cannot isolate problems unique to the challenges
Lack of definitive validity tests	Cannot know when challenges are fully solved
Change inhibits learning	Constantly evolving problems inhibit learning
Every problem is unique	Difficult to employ past solutions
Responsible decision-makers	Humans responsible for successful transformation

Characterize the Nature of the Wicked Problem

What makes the problem at hand wicked? Are there large numbers of different types of stakeholders? Are there inherent conflicts among stakeholder groups? Are there reasons to expect any groups will try to stymie or undermine solutions to the problem? In general, be very honest and clear about likely difficulties.

Identify Anticipated or Experienced Value Deficiencies

What are the value deficiencies, and how are they manifested? Typical examples include performance that is poor, slow, and expensive. Diminished competitive advantage is another, perhaps due to under-investment in new capabilities. Determine whether deficiencies are widely recognized or known only to a few people.

Determine What Processes Need to Be Resigned or Designed

What organizational processes underlie the value deficiencies? How are these processes contributing to the value deficiencies? Do these processes need to be substantially improved or completely replaced?

Identify the stakeholders most aligned with sustaining the status quo.

Engage Stakeholders in How They Would Proceed with Changes

It is essential to involve those stakeholders who will be central to enabling and living with any changes. Seek their insights into the sources of value deficiencies. Solicit their ideas for redesigns or new designs. Make sure that a representative subset of these people is on the team.

Synthesize an Integrated Approach Across Contexts and Time

Consider how alternative solutions will dovetail with contexts (e.g., finance, personnel, operations). Develop staged plans to implement changes over time. Be realistic about the number of stages and time likely needed. Make sure that the whole team understands the staging and timing.

Involve Stakeholders to Support These Changes, Likely Incrementally

Carefully manage stakeholders' expectations of the current stage of implementation so that they do not see this as overwhelming. Inform them that the downstream stages of implementation will be reconsidered and adapted as necessary once the current stage is done.

Secure and Sustain Resources to Accomplish Changes

Make sure that human and financial resources are sufficiently budgeted to be successful. Insufficient budgets will diminish the likelihood of success. Lack of success will undermine stakeholder support. This can easily change the cultural mood from optimism to pessimism.

Execute Changes, Learning along the Way, and Adapting

Execute plans, keeping an eye on lessons learned about hindrances (i.e., things more difficult than expected), and affordances (i.e., things easier than expected). Solicit comments and suggestions on the compilation of lessons learned, including implications for the next stage. Be on the lookout for people with leadership proclivities and leverage their talents for subsequent stages.

Overarching Principles

- Think long term but act short term, creating relatively quick, albeit minor, wins.
- Leverage support of quick wins to enable planning for the next wins.
- Learn from early wins to rethink plans for the next wins.

Possible quick wins addressed in later chapters include increasing reliance on telemedicine in health, increasing high-quality online instruction in education, incentivizing the adoption of renewables in energy, and educating students to identify false information. All of these are happening already and can be leveraged, as well as enhanced.

Complex Adaptive Systems

The nature of behavioral and social phenomena associated with our four challenges is a central consideration. Systems where such phenomena play substantial roles are often considered to belong to a class of systems termed complex adaptive systems (Rouse, 2000, 2008). Systems of this type have the following characteristics:

- They tend to be **nonlinear, dynamic**, and do not inherently reach fixed equilibrium points. The resulting system behaviors may appear to be random or chaotic.
- They are composed of **independent agents** whose behaviors can be described as based on physical, psychological, or social rules, rather than being completely dictated by the physical dynamics of the system.
- Agents' needs or desires, reflected in their rules, are not homogeneous and, therefore, their **goals and behaviors are likely to**

differ or even conflict—these conflicts or competitions tend to lead agents to adapt to each other's behaviors.

- Agents are **intelligent and learn** as they experiment and gain experience, perhaps via "meta" rules, and consequently change behaviors. Thus, overall system properties inherently change over time.
- Adaptation and learning tend to result in **self-organization** and patterns of behavior that emerge rather than being designed into the system. The nature of such emergent behaviors may range from valuable innovations to unfortunate accidents.
- There is **no single point(s) of control**—system behaviors are often unpredictable and uncontrollable, and no one is "in charge." Consequently, the behaviors of complex adaptive systems can usually be influenced more than they can be controlled.

As might be expected, understanding and influencing systems having these characteristics creates significant complications. For example, the use of simulations to represent such systems often does not yield the same results each time they are run. Random variation may lead to varying "tipping points" among stakeholders for different simulation runs. Simulation models can be useful in the exploration of leading indicators of the different tipping points and in assessing potential mitigations for undesirable outcomes.

There are a variety of challenges in addressing complex adaptive systems. The first challenge is to understand the central phenomena that underlie an ecosystem. What are the "physics" of the ecosystem and the rules of the game? Subject matter experts are usually essential to make sure central phenomena are considered and understood.

Second, one needs to understand the stakeholders associated with each of these phenomena. Who are the economic, technical, and user influences? Are there social and political influences? How are influences empowered and resourced? What are their values, concerns, and perceptions?

Third, one needs to understand how to impact the central phenomena. Typically, impacts are through stakeholders or agents. One needs to also understand stakeholders' likely responses to your attempts to impact them. You need to understand how to cultivate positive responses to your initiatives.

Human-Centered Design

The overall approach outlined here requires deciding whose preferences should influence decisions. In some situations, there may be one ultimate decision-maker, although this is very rare in public–private ecosystems. Success usually depends on understanding all stakeholders.

Human-centered design addresses the values, concerns, and perceptions of all stakeholders in designing, developing, deploying, and employing policies, products, and services. The basic idea is to delight primary stakeholders and gain the support of the secondary stakeholders.

This notion first occurred to me at a workshop in the late 1980s at the NASA Langley Research Center near Hampton, Virginia. Many participants were discussing pilot-centered design that focused on enhancing aircraft pilots' abilities, overcoming pilots' limitations, and fostering pilots' acceptance. I suggested that we should do this for all the human stakeholders involved in the success of an aircraft program. People asked what I specifically meant.

I responded, "Pilots may fly them, but they don't build them or buy them!"

In other words, pilots being supportive of design choices may be necessary for success, but it is not sufficient. The airlines have to want to buy the airplanes, the aerospace companies have to be willing to produce them, and regulatory bodies have to certify the use of the planes. The buyers, builders, and regulators have criteria beyond those important to pilots.

I have elaborated on the human-centered design construct and an associated methodology in a book, *Design for Success* (Rouse, 1991).

Two other books soon followed (Rouse, 1992, 1993), addressing innovation and organizational change. The human-centered design methodology has been applied many times and continually refined (Rouse, 2007, 2015, 2019).

The premise of human-centered design is that the major stakeholders need to perceive policies, products, and services to be valid, acceptable, and viable. Valid policies, products, and services demonstrably help solve the problems for which they are intended. Acceptable policies, products, and services solve problems in ways that stakeholders prefer. Viable policies, products, and services provide benefits that are worth the costs of use. Costs here include the efforts needed to learn and use policies, products, and services, not just the purchase price.

The overall approach presented here is intended to increase validity, acceptability, and viability beyond that usually experienced with the ways in which problems of the scope addressed in this book are usually pursued. This begs the question of what shortcomings plague existing approaches.

First and foremost are viability issues. Sponsors of change initiatives complain that they take too long and are too expensive. This is due in part to the business processes of sponsors. However, more fundamentally, much time and money go into developing aspects of policies that, at least in retrospect, were not needed to address the questions of primary interest.

Second are acceptability issues. Many key stakeholders in the types of challenges addressed in this book are not educated in analytic methods and tools. Nevertheless, they are often highly talented, have considerable influence, and will not accept that the optimal policy, somehow magically produced, is X equals 12. We need methods and tools that are more engaging for these types of stakeholders (Rouse, 2014b).

Third are validity issues. There is often concern that overall analyses are of questionable validity (Rouse, 2015, 2019). This concern is due in part to the possibility that assumptions are inconsistent across component analyses. There is also the issue of incompatible definitions of organizational states across component analyses, which can lead to misleading or incorrect results. This is particularly plaguing when one is unaware of these incompatibilities.

The overall approach outlined earlier overcomes these issues in several ways. The early steps of the methodology focus on problem formulation, with particular emphasis on interactive pruning of the problem space prior to any in-depth explorations. In-depth analyses tend to be expensive, so it is important to be sure they are warranted.

Second, we have found that key stakeholders value being immersed in interactive visualizations of the phenomena, and relationships among phenomena associated with their domain and the questions of interest. This enables them to manipulate controls and explore responses. This is typically done in a group setting with much discussion and debate.

Third, the overall approach explicitly addresses agreeing on a consistent set of assumptions across analyses. This prompts delving into the underpinnings of each type of analysis. The overarching question is whether connecting multiple types of analysis will yield results that are valid in the context of the questions at hand.

Stakeholders

Who are the stakeholders in the four challenges? Table 2.2 provides a good sampling, although it is inevitable that key players are missing. The central point, however, is that addressing the challenges involves an enormous range of stakeholders whose values, concerns, and perceptions have to be understood and addressed if interventions are to be successful. I have found that even a single key stakeholder who is dead set against the changes being considered can stymie an initiative.

Attributes

What do stakeholders care about? In other words, what are the attributes they will use to assess the utility of each alternative?

Table 2.2 Stakeholders Versus Challenges

Stakeholder	Challenge				
	Population Health	Lifelong Education	Energy and Climate	Mis/Disinformation
Constituencies	Congress, patients, families, employers	Congress, students, parents, employers	Congress, public	Congress, public, employers
Government agencies	HHS, MHS, VHA, states, cities	DOE, states, cities	DOE, EPA, NOAA, FEMA, States, Cities	DOD, DHS, IC, CMS
Agencies workforce	Employees, unions	Employees, unions	Employees, unions	Employees, unions
Industry and institutions	Providers, payers, suppliers	Institutions, publishers, suppliers	Coal, oil, gas companies, and related services	Social media companies, influencers, advertisers
Industry workforce	Employees, unions	Employees, unions	Employees, unions	Employees, unions
Oversight organizations	Accreditation and licensing organizations, AHA, et al.	Accreditation and licensing organizations, AHEE	FERC, AEOA, GAO	DHS, FDA, FCC
Advocacy groups	NAHAC, Cancer Society, Heart Assoc., et al.	Learning Disabilities, Education Trust, Stand for Children, et al.	Nature Conservancy, World Wide Fund for Nature, et al.	American Civil Liberties Union, Free Speech Alliance,

Table 2.3 Challenges Versus Attributes

Challenge	Attributes		
	Validity	Acceptability	Viability
Population health	Proposed interventions are evidence-based and supported by key stakeholders	Proposed interventions are aligned with healthcare values and norms	Educational and economic benefits of change outweigh costs of change
Lifelong education	Proposed interventions will have desired educational impacts	Proposed interventions are aligned with educational values and norms	Educational benefits of change outweigh costs of change
Energy and climate	Impacts of proposed interventions are clear and believed	Proposed interventions are aligned with domain values and norms	Climate benefits outweigh costs of change
Mis/ Disinformation	Proposed interventions mitigate mis/dis without violating First Amendment rights	Proposed interventions can be accommodated within current practices	Benefits of mis/dis mitigation outweigh costs of execution

Table 2.3 provides a high-level definition of attributes for each ecosystem. These high-level definitions become much more specific in Chapter 3.

Analytic Framework

Figure 2.1 shows how we bring all the human-centered design concepts together. This representation embodies the principles of human-centered design, built around Set-Based Design (Sobek, Ward, & Liker, 1999), Quality Function Deployment (Hauser & Clausing, 1988), and Design Structure Matrices (Eppinger & Browning, 2012). Multi-stakeholder, multi-attribute utility theory

(Keeney & Raiffa, 1993) is used to project the value of alternatives. Note that validity, acceptability, and viability in Figure 2.1 are defined in the aforementioned discussion of human-centered design.

Sobek, Ward, and Liker (1999) contrast set-based design (SBD) with point-based design. Developed by Toyota, SBD considers a broader range of possible designs and delays certain decisions longer. They argue that, "Taking time up front to explore and document feasible solutions from design and manufacturing perspectives leads to tremendous gains in efficiency and product integration later in the process and for subsequent development cycles."

SBD is reflected in Figure 2.1 in terms of defining and elaborating multiple solutions, including those of competitors or adversaries. Quality function deployment (Hauser & Clausing, 1988) translates the "voice of the customer" into engineering characteristics. For

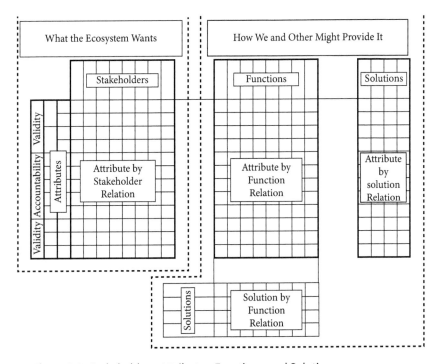

Figure 2.1 Stakeholders, Attributes, Functions, and Solutions

Figure 2.1, this translates into "voices of the stakeholders." Design structure matrices (Eppinger & Browning, 2012) are used to model the structure of complex systems or processes. In Figure 2.1, multiple models are maintained to represent alternative offerings, as well as current and anticipated competitors' offerings.

The "What the Ecosystem Wants" section of Figure 2.1 characterizes the stakeholders in the solution (e.g., a policy or regulation), and their utility functions associated with context-specific attributes clustered in terms of validity, acceptability, and viability. The section of Figure 2.1 labeled "How We and Others Might Provide It" specifies, on the right, the attribute values associated with each solution. The functions associated with each solution are defined on the left of this section. Functions are things like steering, accelerating, and braking, as well as functions that may not be available in all solutions (e.g., backup camera). For policy analyses, functions might involve, for example, fuel efficiency targets, penalties for missing targets, and communications and educational offerings.

Attribute to function relationships in Figure 2.1 are expressed on a somewhat arbitrary scale from −3 to +3. Positive numbers indicate that improving a function increases the attribute. Negative numbers indicate that improving a function decreases an attribute. For example, a backup camera may increase the price of the vehicle but decrease insurance costs. The penalty levels in a policy may increase compliance, unless the economic costs of compliance are not sustainable. These relationships are of use for projecting where improvements are most likely to pay off.

Solutions on the bottom of Figure 2.1 are composed of functions, which are related to attributes of interest to stakeholders. In keeping with the principles of set-based design, multiple solutions are pursued in parallel, including potential offerings by adversaries or competitors. While it is typical for one solution to be selected for major investment—while others may secure lesser investments—the representations of all solutions are retained, quite often being reused for subsequent opportunities.

Using the framework provided by Figure 2.1, and principles from SBD, QFD, DSM, and others, one can create multi-attribute models of how alternatives address the values, concerns, and perceptions of all the stakeholders in designing, developing, manufacturing, buying, and using policies, products, and services. We also need to consider the likely uncertainties associated with the attributes of the alternatives.

The expected utility of an alternative can be defined as the utility of the outcomes a solution provides times the probability that these outcomes will result (Keeney & Raiffa, 1993). The probability may be discrete, or it may be represented as a probability density function. For the former, the calculation involves multiplication and summation; for the latter, the calculation involves integration. The mechanics of these calculations are explained in a recent book (Rouse, 2022).

We can employ a computational instantiation of Figure 2.1 to explore alternative solutions. While one or more alternatives may seem to predominate, people typically want to understand how alternative assumptions affect this dominance. For example, they may see that alternative X prevails with particular assumptions, while alternative Y may seem stronger with another set of assumptions. I have found that insightful decision-makers will then turn to the group and ask, "What creative changes could we make so that these two outcomes are not so different?"

This analytic platform then becomes a means for exploring various "what if?" scenarios. What if agency A provided agency B with a subsidy for enabling particular outcomes? But, that's illegal. Okay, but we can address that later. Could that make the difference in this impasse? The abilities to mutually and creatively explore "what if?" questions are often the key to new futures. I explore this in depth in Chapter 5.

Conclusions

In this chapter, I explored concepts, principles, and models from the behavioral and social sciences. This rich knowledge base differs greatly from the physical sciences. Behavioral and social systems are laced with complexity, uncertainty, ambiguity, and non-repeatability. One can influence them but cannot control outcomes as one often can with a physical system.

I characterized the challenges of such systems as wicked problems. I generalized the notion of wicked problems using a framework of complex adaptive systems. The phenomena associated with such systems require a highly nuanced and deep approach to understanding the agents in such systems. This can be accomplished using a human-centered design framework focused on the values, concerns, and perceptions of all the stakeholders in the challenge being addressed.

With our conceptual and methodological underpinnings in place, we now need to dive into the details of the ecosystems surrounding our four challenges. This will enable an understanding of how the knowledge, theories, and methods discussed in this chapter can facilitate progress in addressing these challenges.

References

Blinder, A.S. (2013). *After the Music Stopped: The Financial Crisis, the Response, and the Work Ahead*. New York: Penguin.

Castells, M. (1996). *Rise of the Network Society*. Malden, MA: Blackwell.

DeLong, J.B. (2022). *Slouching Towards Utopia: An Economic History of the Twentieth Century*. New York: Basic Books.

Edsall, T.B. (2022). Why Aren't You Voting in Your Financial Self-Interest? *New York Times*, September 14.

Edwards, W., & Tversky, A. (Eds.) (1967). *Decision Making*. New York: Penguin.

Eppinger, S.D., & Browning, T.R. (2012). *Design Structure Matrix Methods and Applications*. Cambridge, MA: MIT Press.

Giddens, A. (1979). *Central Problems in Social Theory: Action, Structure and Contradictions in Social Analysis*. Berkeley, CA: University of California Press.

Gordon, R.J. (2016). *The Rise and Fall of American Growth: The U.S. Standard of Living Since the Civil War*. Princeton, NJ: Princeton University Press.

Habermas, J. (1988). *Structural Transformation of the Public Sphere.* Cambridge, MA: MIT-Press.

Haidt, J. (2022). Why the past 10 years of American life have been uniquely stupid: It's not just a phase. *The Atlantic,* April.

Haidt, J.R., & Rose-Stockwell, T. (2019). The dark psychology of social networks: Why it feels like everything has gone haywire. *The Atlantic,* December.

Hauser, J.R., & Clausing, D. (1988, May–June). The house of quality. *Harvard Business Review,* 66 (3), 63–73.

Kahneman, D. (2011). *Thinking, Fast and Slow.* New York: Farrar, Straus and Giroux.

Keeney, R.L., & Raiffa, H. (1993). *Decisions with Multiple Objectives: Preference and Value Tradeoffs.* Cambridge, UK: Cambridge University Press.

Khanna, R. (2022). *Dignity in a Digital Age: Making Tech Work for All of Us.* New York: Simon & Schuster.

Klein, E. (2020). *Why We Are Polarized.* New York: Simon & Schuster.

Klein, G. (2004). *The Power of Intuition: How to Use Your Gut Feelings to Make Better Decisions at Work.* New York: Currency.

Leonhardt, D. (2022). A crisis is coming: The twin threats to American democracy. *New York Times,* September 17.

Lewis, M. (2011). *The Big Short: Inside the Doomsday Machine.* New York: Norton.

Luhmann, N. (1995). *Social Systems.* Stanford, CA: Stanford University Press.

Marble, W., & Nall, C. (2021). Where self-interest trumps ideology: Liberal homeowners and local opposition to housing development. *The Journal of Politics,* 83 (4), https://doi.org/10.1086/711717.

Miller, G.A. (1956). The magical number seven, plus or minus two: Some limits on our capacity for processing information. *Psychological Review,* 63 (2), 81–97.

Mintzberg, H. (1975). The manager's job: Folklore and fact. *Harvard Business Review,* July–August.

Mokyr, J. (1992). *The Lever of Riches: Technological Creativity and Economic Progress.* Oxford, UK: Oxford University Press.

Norman, A. (2021). *Mental Immunity: Infectious Ideas, Mind-Parasites, and the Search for a Better Way to Think.* New York: Harper.

Polanyi, K. (1944). *The Great Transformation—The Political and Economic Origins of Our Time*. New York: Farrar & Rinehart.

Rittel, H.W. J., & Webber, M.M. (1973). Dilemmas in a general theory of planning. *Policy Sciences*, 4 (2), 155–169.

Rose, T. (2022). *Collective Illusions: Conformity, Complicity, and the Science of Why We Make Bad Decisions*. New York: Hachette.

Rosenberg, I. (2021). *The Fight for Free Speech: Ten Cases that Define Our First Amendment Freedoms*. New York: New York University Press.

Rouse, W.B. (1991). *Design or Success: A Human-Centered Approach to Designing Successful Products and Systems*. New York: Wiley.

Rouse, W.B. (1992). *Strategies for Innovation: Creating Successful Products, Systems, and Organizations*. New York: Wiley.

Rouse, W.B. (1993). *Catalysts for Change: Concepts and Principles for Enabling Innovation*. New York: Wiley.

Rouse, W.B. (1998). *Don't Jump to Solutions: Thirteen Delusions that Undermine Strategic Thinking*. San Francisco: Jossey-Bass.

Rouse, W.B. (2000). Managing complexity: Disease control as a complex adaptive system. *Information-Knowledge-Systems Management*, 2 (2), 143–165.

Rouse, W.B. (2007). *People and Organizations: Explorations of Human-Centered Design*. New York: Wiley.

Rouse, W.B. (2008). Healthcare as a complex adaptive system: Implications for design and management. *The Bridge*, 38 (1), 17–25.

Rouse, W.B. (Ed.) (2010). *The Economics of Human Systems Integration: Valuation of Investments in People's Training and Education, Safety and Health, and Work Productivity*. New York: John Wiley.

Rouse, W.B. (2014a). *A Century of Innovation: From Wooden Sailing Ships to Electric Railways, Computers, Space Travel and Internet*. Raleigh, NC: Lulu Press.

Rouse, W.B. (2014b). Human interaction with policy flight simulators. *Journal of Applied Ergonomics*, 45 (1), 72–77.

Rouse, W.B. (2015). *Modeling and Visualization of Complex Systems and Enterprises: Explorations of Physical, Human, Economic, and Social Phenomena*. Hoboken, NJ: John Wiley.

Rouse, W.B. (2019). *Computing Possible Futures: Model-Based Explorations of "What if?"* Oxford, UK: Oxford University Press.

Rouse, W.B. (2022). *Transforming Public-Private Ecosystems: Understanding and Enabling Innovation in Complex Systems.* Oxford, UK: Oxford University Press.

Rouse, W.B., Johns, M.M.E., & Stead, W.W. (2022). *Medical Misinformation & Disinformation.* Washington, DC: McCourt School of Public Policy, Georgetown University.

Sage, A.P., & Rouse, W.B. (2011). *Economic System Analysis and Assessment.* New York: Wiley.

Simon, H.A. (1957). *Models of Man: Social and Rational.* New York: Wiley.

Simon, H.A. (1969). *The Sciences of the Artificial.* Cambridge, MA: MIT Press.

Simon, H.A. (1972). Theories of bounded rationality. In C.B. McGuire & R. Radner, Eds., *Decision and Organization* (Chap. 8), pp. 161–176. New York: North Holland.

Singer, P.W., & Brooking, E.T. (2018). *Like War: The Weaponization of Social Media.* Boston, MA: Houghton Mifflin.

Sobek, D.K., Ward, A.C., & Liker, J.K. (1999). Toyota's principles of set-based concurrent engineering. *Sloan Management Review*, 40 (2), 67–83.

Thaler, R.H. (2015). *Misbehaving: The Making of Behavioral Economics.* New York: Norton.

Thaler, R.H., & Sunstein, C.R. (2009). *Nudge: Improving Decisions about Health, Wealth, and Happiness.* New York: Penguin.

Wapshott, N. (2011). *Keynes Hayek: The Clash that Defined Modern Economics.* New York: Norton.

Zegart, A.B. (2022). *Spies, Lies & Algorithms: The History and Future of American Intelligence.* Princeton, NJ: Princeton University Press.

3
Insights for Addressing Challenges

Stakeholders, Attributes, and Preferences

Introduction

To address the types of phenomena discussed in Chapter 2, we need to engage reality as it is rather than what we tend to assume or hope it is. The fundamental question concerns what evidence-based knowledge is available for understanding the physical, behavioral, and social phenomena underlying the challenges at hand. Addressing this question requires conducting rigorous evidence-based analyses of underlying phenomena and alternative courses of action.

Table 3.1 illustrates the range of topics addressed in this chapter. Succinctly, the focus is on the phenomena underlying the four societal challenges, as well as the forces driving these phenomena. This both illustrates the thinking required and provides a basis for continuing the pursuit of these challenges.

A fundamental question concerns where change interventions should be targeted. As discussed earlier, several questions should guide these choices:

- Will the benefits envisioned be embraced by stakeholders?
- Is any stakeholder organization currently providing these benefits?
- Are they successfully providing these benefits?
- Is the scope of those benefited limited by resources or mandates?
- What might hinder the broad provision of these benefits?

Beyond Quick Fixes. William B. Rouse, Oxford University Press. © William B. Rouse (2023).
DOI: 10.1093/oso/9780198892533.003.0003

Table 3.1 Insights into Challenges

Attributes	Challenges			
	Population Health	Lifelong Education	Energy and Climate	Mis/Dis Information
Underlying physical, behavioral and social phenomena	Disease, prevention, treatment	Learning, practicing, experiencing, collaborating	Emissions of carbon, methane, and so on	Rumoring, deception, manipulation, trust
Delivery of associated goods and services	Providers, payers, suppliers (e.g., drugs and devices)	Schools, colleges publishers	Extraction, conversion, transmission, distribution, consumption	Social media, broadcast media, Internet more broadly
Effectiveness of delivery ecosystem	Inadequate information sharing and care coordination; misaligned incentives	Inadequate communication and support of educational best practices	Inadequate renewable energy sources; solar, wind, hydro, nuclear; infrastructure	Inadequate societal immunity system that requires evidence to support beliefs
Beneficiaries of delivery ecosystem	Patients, 16 million employees, companies, shareholders	Students, 15 million employees, companies, shareholders	Everyone, 7 million employees, companies, shareholders	Advertisers, politicians, pundits
Societal values and norms	Health as a public vs. private good	Education as a public vs. private good	Freedom of choice	Freedom of speech

In this chapter, I provide the background that will enable answering these questions for the four challenges in Chapters 4 and 5. My perspective on these issues is very pragmatic in terms of strategies and plans for formulating interventions and deploying them.

Population Health

As I elaborate later in this section, population health involves the integration of health, education, and social services to keep a defined population healthy, to address health challenges holistically, and to assist with the realities of being mortal (Rouse, Johns, & Pepe, 2017, 2019). To understand why this is an enormous challenge, I first need to describe the realities of the US healthcare delivery system.

Steadily increasing costs, long waiting times, an aging population, declining reimbursements, and a fragmented system are how many people characterize healthcare in the US. In addition, the Affordable Care Act (ACA) has caused a transformation of the healthcare industry. This industry also involves complicated relationships among patients, physicians, hospitals, health plans, pharmaceutical companies, healthcare equipment companies, and government.

Figure 3.1 depicts the intricacy of the US healthcare system, with immense numbers of complex interconnections. It suggests that stakeholders' strategic decisions—for example, healthcare providers' plans, health insurance reimbursement schemes, and preventive healthcare initiatives will experience both positive and negative—and often, unforeseen—consequences. Because of this complexity, even proactive decision-makers who thoroughly game out what might happen can easily fail to anticipate how various actors or competitors will respond. Methods drawing upon significant insights into decision-making processes are needed (Rouse & Cortese, 2010; Rouse & Serban, 2014).

Among the stakeholders in the complex US healthcare system, hospitals are dominant players, with significant contributions to the overall economy. Because of the uncertainties associated with the US healthcare system, it is quite understandable that

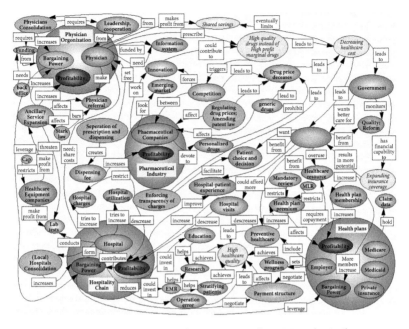

Figure 3.1   Healthcare Ecosystem (Yu, Rouse, Serban, & Veral, 2016)

hospitals are uncertain about how they should best respond to pressures and opportunities. This is particularly relevant for hospitals located in competitive metropolitan areas such as New York City, where more than fifty hospital corporations are competing, among which many are the nation's best. Questions that arise in this uncertain environment include:

- What if we wait until the healthcare market stabilizes and, in the near term, only invest in operational efficiency?
- Should we merge with competing hospitals to decrease competition and increase negotiating power with payers and suppliers?
- Should we mainly focus on acquiring physician practices in highly reimbursed diagnostic groups?

Aggregated decisions from numerous hospitals could change the future hospital market, potentially affecting the cost and quality of delivered services. The diagram in Figure 3.1 was the starting point

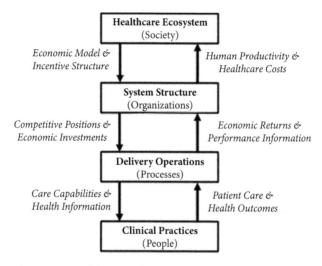

Figure 3.2 Healthcare Delivery Ecosystem

for developing an agent-based model of the New York City healthcare delivery ecosystem to explore likely merger and acquisition scenarios (Yu, Rouse, Serban, & Veral, 2016).

Figure 3.2 shows the healthcare delivery ecosystem. Patients and clinicians interact at the People level. The Process level provides capabilities and information that enable care and outcomes. The Organization level includes entities that invest in capabilities and compete for economic returns. Society defines the rules of the game and expects a healthy and productive population, within acceptable costs. My later expansion of this depiction to include population health will significantly increase complexity.

Stakeholders

Table 3.2 lists classes of stakeholders and examples. Expanding a few of these categories of stakeholders, the number of stakeholders becomes substantially larger.

There are over one million physicians in the US, over 6,000 hospitals, over 600 health systems, and 3,700 local public health agencies. All of these entities have significant discretion in their priorities and

Table 3.2 Stakeholders in Healthcare Delivery

Stakeholders	Examples
Constituencies	Congress, patients, families, employers
Government agencies	HHS, MHS, VHA, states, cities
Agencies workforce	Employees, unions
Industry and institutions	Providers, payers, suppliers
Industry workforce	Employees, unions
Oversight organizations	Accreditation and licensing orgs., AHA, et al.
Advocacy groups	NAHAC, Cancer Society, Heart Assoc., et al.

HHS = Dept. of Health and Human Serv.; MHS = Military Health System; VHA = Veterans Health Admin.; AHA = American Hospital Assoc.; NAHAC = National Assoc. of Healthcare Advocacy

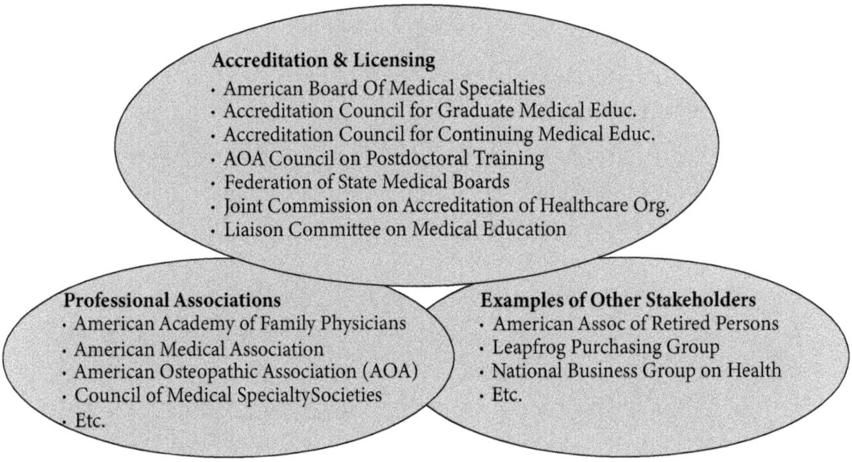

Accreditation & Licensing
· American Board Of Medical Specialties
· Accreditation Council for Graduate Medical Educ.
· Accreditation Council for Continuing Medical Educ.
· AOA Council on Postdoctoral Training
· Federation of State Medical Boards
· Joint Commission on Accreditation of Healthcare Org.
· Liaison Committee on Medical Education

Professional Associations
· American Academy of Family Physicians
· American Medical Association
· American Osteopathic Association (AOA)
· Council of Medical SpecialtySocieties
· Etc.

Examples of Other Stakeholders
· American Assoc of Retired Persons
· Leapfrog Purchasing Group
· National Business Group on Health
· Etc.

Figure 3.3 Key Stakeholders in the Medical Community

allocation of resources. These represent the people and organizations that deliver health services.

Figure 3.3 lists representative stakeholders in the processes of accreditation and licensing, professional associations, advocacy groups, and business groups. Two observations are of particular note. First, each US state addresses clinician licensing in its own way—there is no national clinician license. Second, there are over 1,200 recognized patient advocacy groups in the US.

Clearly, the healthcare delivery ecosystem in the US is very complex. I have often characterized it as a federation of millions of entrepreneurs without no one in charge. I have found that every audience relates to this characterization.

Population Health

As defined earlier, population health involves integration of health, education, and social services to keep a defined population healthy, to address health challenges holistically, and to assist with the realities of being mortal. Consequently, population health involves a wide range of interventions/services, many of which are not traditionally associated with the healthcare system in Figures 3.1 and 3.2. Figure 3.4 portrays who is involved in providing this wide range of services and the inherent difficulty of accessing these services in the US.

There are many entrenched rice bowls in healthcare in terms of providers, payers, pharma, and others. However, Social Security

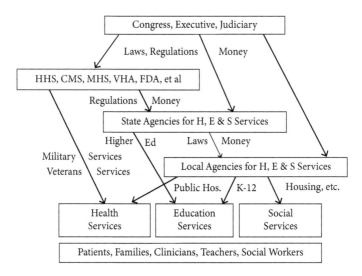

Figure 3.4 Relationships Among Organizations and Services

provided a highly valued benefit in 1935 and did not disrupt existing rice bowls. My sense is that mental health, as a broadly defined public health challenge, is not as sclerotic. Consequently, nationwide federal investment in standards, guidelines, and treatment might be welcomed.

Lifelong Education

In the US, there are 49.5 million students and 3.7 million teachers in K-12; 19.4 million students and 1.5 million faculty at colleges and universities; 131,000 K-12 schools and almost 4,000 colleges and universities. Of particular significance, there are 14,000 local school boards, each of which has discretion over the programs and budgets of public schools in their districts. Consequently, the heterogeneity of K-12 programs across the US is quite significant.

Amidst this complexity, this challenge concerns assuring lifelong education for all people in the US, from pre-K to older adults needing new knowledge and skills to manage their golden years. We need greater consistency of educational requirements and programs so that the educational pipeline can be better managed and resourced, and employers can have reasonable expectations of what particular credentials mean. For example, nationwide federal investment in STEM (science, technology, engineering, and math) and STW (skilled technical workforce) in terms of standards, guidelines, and curricula might be welcomed, particularly in communities challenged to perform.

Education strongly interacts with other challenges. Level of education is correlated with health as well as income, which is also correlated with health. In energy, nationwide federal investments in renewables, Generation 3 nuclear, storage, and transmission are already major commitments; workforce retraining, not so much. In mis/disinformation, nationwide federal policies will predominate. Education on information management and mental immunity initiatives will be locally delivered.

Higher Education

For this challenge, I have devoted significant attention to higher education. Figure 3.5 provides a schematic view of the ecosystem of higher education. Schools are, of course, central, with primary and secondary schools feeding higher education. Students transition from schools to employers. Employers provide payrolls to employees and taxes to government. Government provides money as well as policies and regulations. Government money includes grants to schools, government-backed loans, and scholarships and grants. Family resources are also central.

Schools employ money to pay faculty members and staff, create and maintain infrastructure, acquire textbooks and other publications, and pay for various services. Schools are managed by Boards of Trustees for private institutions, or Boards of Regents or

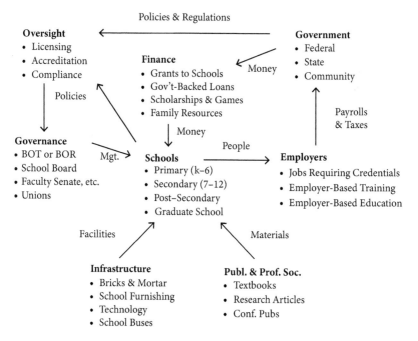

Figure 3.5 The Ecosystem of Higher Education

equivalent for public institutions. Faculty Senates, or equivalent, oversee curricula, faculty recruitment, and promotions. Unions play central roles at some institutions.

Oversight is influenced by government policies and regulations. Licensing and accreditation organizations play central roles, often with regional or national organizations exercising oversight. Compliance functions have increasingly become central at most institutions. Faculty and staff members often spend significant time adhering to compliance policies and procedures.

Figure 3.5 mainly serves to provide the broad context within which individual institutions have to operate. Figure 3.6 depicts a multi-level architecture of academic enterprises in higher education (Rouse, 2016). The practices of education, research, and service occur in the context of processes, structures, and ecosystems. Understanding the relationships among practices, processes, structure, and ecosystem provides the basis for transforming academia, leveraging its strengths, and overcoming its limitations.

The architecture in Figure 3.6 helps us to understand how various elements of the enterprise system either enable or hinder other elements of the system, all of which are embedded in a complex behavioral and social ecosystem. Practices are much more efficient and effective when enabled by well-articulated and supported processes for delivering capabilities and associated information, as well as capturing and disseminating outcomes.

Processes exist to the extent that organizations (i.e., campuses, colleges, schools, and departments) invest in them. These investments are influenced by economic models and incentive structures, and are made in pursuit of competitive positions and economic returns. These forces hopefully coalesce to create an educated and productive population, at an acceptable cost.

When we employ Figure 3.6 to understand relationships among universities, the interesting phenomenon in Figure 3.7 emerges. The hierarchical structure of Figure 3.6 dovetails with the heterarchical nature of academic disciplines. The dotted rectangle in Figure 3.7 represents how faculty disciplines both compete and define standards across universities.

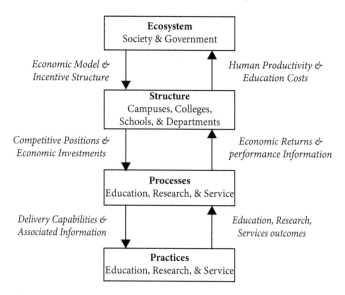

Figure 3.6 Multi-Level Architecture of Academic Enterprises

The disciplines define the agenda for "normal" science and technology, including valued sponsors of this agenda and valued outlets for research results. Members of faculty disciplines at other universities have an enormous impact on promotion and tenure processes at any particular university. Such professional affiliations also affect other types of enterprises, for example, healthcare. However, universities seem to be the only enterprise that allows external parties to largely determine who gets promoted and tenured internally. This has substantial impacts on understanding the performance of any particular university.

More specifically, the standards set at the discipline level determine:

- Agenda for "normal" science and technology
- Valued sponsors of this agenda
- Valued outlets for research results

Consequently, almost everyone chases the same sponsors and journals, leading to decreasing probabilities of success with either. In

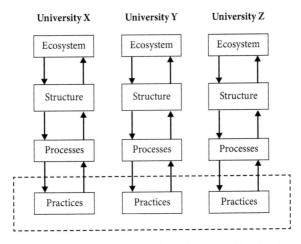

Figure 3.7 Hybrid Multi-Level Architecture of Academia

addition, each faculty member produces another faculty member every year or so, swelling the ranks of the competitors. Recently, retirements are being delayed to refill individuals' retirement coffers, which decreases the numbers of open faculty slots.

As the probabilities of success decrease, faculty members:

- Write an increasing number of proposals
- Submit an increasing number of journal articles
- Resulting in constantly increasing costs of success
- Congested pipelines, which foster constantly increasing times until success
- The bottom line is less success, greater costs, and longer delays.

The economic model of research universities discussed in one of the case studies later in this chapter enables the exploration of these phenomena.

Universities can hold off these consequences by hiring fewer tenure-track faculty members (i.e., using teaching faculty and adjuncts). But this will retard their march up the rankings and hence slow the acquisition of talented students, who will succeed in life and later reward the institution with gifts and endowments. I later explore the tradeoff between controlling cost and enhancing brand value.

Alternatively, universities can pursue "niche dominance" and only hire tenure-track faculty in areas where they can leapfrog to excellence. This will, unfortunately, result in two classes of faculty—those on the fast track to excellence and those destined to heavy teaching loads. The first class will be paid a lot more because of the great risks of their being attracted away to enhance other universities' brands.

Stakeholders

Table 3.3 lists classes of stakeholders and examples. Expanding a few of these categories of stakeholders, the number of stakeholders becomes substantially larger.

Figure 3.6 indicates a wide range of stakeholders beyond faculty members and students. In fact, increases in numbers of non-faculty staff members and administrators have been the primary drivers of increased costs of higher education (Rouse, 2016). Figure 3.7 depicts central relationships among universities. Faculty members

Table 3.3 Stakeholders in Education

Stakeholders	Examples
Constituencies	Congress, students, parents, employers
Government agencies	Federal, state, and city departments of education, school boards
Agencies workforce	Employees, unions
Industry and institutions	Institutions, trustees, regents, publishers, suppliers
Industry workforce	Employees, unions
Oversight organizations	Accreditation and licensing organizations, AHEE
Advocacy groups	Learning disabilities, education trust, stand for children, and so on

AHEE = Association for Higher Education Effectiveness

within each discipline at a particular university are evaluated for promotion and tenure by faculty members in each discipline at other universities. More specifically, universities effectively outsource the evaluation of their faculty members to other universities.

Faculty members know this and invest considerable time building relationships with faculty members at other institutions that will later be evaluating them. The very expensive process of preparing and submitting research articles is central to this distributed evaluation process. Consequently, one could argue that considerable resources only indirectly benefit students.

However, the reputation or brand value of a university is central to attracting the best students. Brand value is highly correlated with faculty members' publications and reputations. Consequently, university leaders have to struggle with tradeoffs in investing in brand value and the implications of these investments in overall costs (Rouse, Lombardi, & Craig, 2018).

K-12 Education

The success of higher education is critically dependent on the preparation of students in K-12, which in turn depends on pre-K. The quality of this system throughout the US is highly uneven. As with healthcare, we spend a lot to achieve poor results compared to other OECD countries. The fragmentation of education in the US hinders agreeing on best practices and widely adopting them.

Public K-12 education is, for the most part, financed by local property taxes. Consequently, the level of resources available depends on the value of the properties in the school district. The result is that poorer people have poorer schools. Schools in wealthier school districts, and private schools in those districts, have more resources, and often more highly engaged parents.

The social determinants of health and education tend to trap poorer people into patterns of low performance. People are ill-prepared to break out and move up. For example, it is impossible to become STEM-ready if your K-12 schools do not offer the requisite high school STEM courses. More profoundly, if a child does not achieve a third-grade reading level by the time they finish that grade, chances are that they will never go to college. Thus, a nine-year-old boy or girl is behind the eight ball already.

Energy and Climate

There are 3,300 utilities and 9,000 oil and natural gas companies, employing over 5 million people. The energy and climate ecosystem is clearly the most pervasive discussed thus far. Everyone is a user of energy, every day. I begin by looking at the overall system that needs to be influenced. This broad perspective can facilitate addressing the challenges of climate change and its likely consequences.

As shown in Figure 3.8, the earth can be considered as a collection of different phenomena operating on different time scales (Rouse, 2014). Loosely speaking, there are four interconnected systems: environment, population, industry, and government. In this notional model, the population consumes resources from the

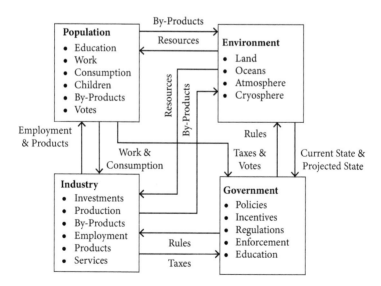

Figure 3.8 Earth as a System

environment and creates by-products. Industry also consumes resources and creates by-products, but it also produces employment. The government collects taxes and produces rules. The use of the environment is influenced by those rules.

Each system component has a different associated time constant. In the case of the environment, the time constant is decades to centuries. The population's time constant can be as short as weeks to months, as the pandemic has illustrated. The government's time constant is longer, thinking in terms of years. Industry is longer still, on the order of decades. These systems can be represented at different levels of abstraction and/or aggregation, as shown in Figure 3.9. The levels of this ecosystem have fairly well-entrenched perceptions and priorities:

- *Society*: Elected officials have great difficulty trading off short-term versus long-term costs and benefits, due to a large extent to the concerns, values, and perceptions of their constituents—citizens and companies.

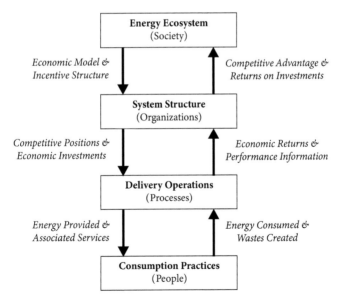

Figure 3.9 Ecosystem of Energy and Climate

- *Organizations*: The vested interests in energy extraction, refinement, and use are enormous and are naturally inclined to sustain status quo business models, and the benefits these models provide to these organizations.
- *Processes*: Processes for extracting, refining, and utilizing fossil fuels are well developed, employ millions of people, and represent trillions of dollars of stock market capitalization.
- *People*: People have long exploited natural resources and come to depend on the benefits of these resources in terms of both consumption and employment. Changing consumption habits is very difficult.

The hierarchical representation of Figure 3.9 does not capture the fact that this is a highly distributed system, with all elements interconnected. It is difficult to solve one part of the problem, as it affects other pieces. By-products are related to population size, so one way to reduce by-products is to moderate population growth. Technology may help to ameliorate some of the by-products and their effects, but it is also possible that technology could exacerbate the effects. Clean technologies lower by-product rates but tend to increase overall use, for instance.

Sentient stakeholders include population, industry, and government. Gaining these stakeholders' support for such decisions will depend upon the credibility of the predictions of behavior, at all levels in the system. Central to this support are "space value" and "time value" discount rates. The consequences that are closest in space and time to stakeholders matter the most and have lower discount rates; attributes more distributed in time and space are more highly discounted. These discount rates will differ across stakeholders.

People will also try to "game" any strategy to improve the system, seeking to gain a share of the resources being invested in executing any transformation strategy. The way to deal with that is to make the system sufficiently transparent to understand the game being played. Sometimes gaming the system will actually be an innovation; other times, prohibitions of the specific gaming tactics will be needed.

The phenomena of central interest are depicted in Figure 3.10. Climate change is affecting the weather. More specifically, human behaviors are affecting the climate in terms of increased global warming and increased temperatures are affecting the weather.

There are official definitions of climate and weather as provided by the National Weather Service:

> Weather is defined as the state of the atmosphere at a given time and place, with respect to variables such as temperature, moisture, wind speed and direction, and barometric pressure. Climate is defined as the expected frequency of specific states of the atmosphere, ocean, and land, including variables such as temperature (land, ocean, and atmosphere), salinity (oceans), soil moisture (land), wind speed and direction (atmosphere), current strength and direction (oceans). Climate encompasses the weather over different periods of time and also relates to mutual interactions between the components of the earth system (e.g., atmospheric composition, volcanic eruptions, changes in the earth's orbit around the sun, changes in the energy from the sun itself). (NWS, 2020)

The impacts on weather are no longer hypothetical. We are already at climate tipping points in terms of arctic warming, ice collapses, and ocean heat waves. There are emerging consequences for US national parks in terms of climate change and invasive species, as well as overcrowding and money woes. The consequences of global warming are no longer hypothetical.

There are numerous flood mitigation efforts across the US and concerns about the cost effectiveness of mitigation. Climate restoration is also being addressed. As compelling as such proposals may be, they face fundamental economic hurdles. The implications are clear. We cannot deal with global warming by simply restoring everything that is damaged, and then restoring it again after the next flood, for example. We either have to stem the use of fossil fuels or prepare for disruptive and eventually very different living conditions.

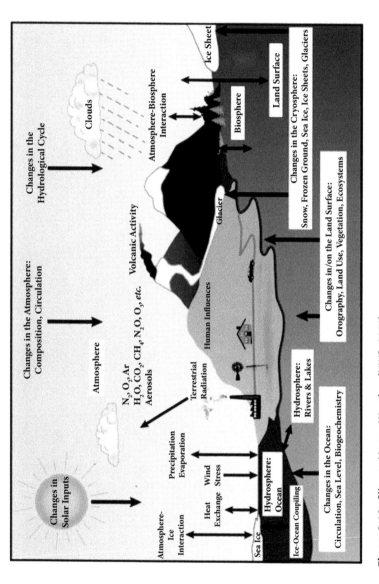

Figure 3.10 Climate Versus Weather (NWS, 2020)

https://www.weather.gov/climateservices/CvW, Accessed 11-16-20.

On a longer term, it is projected that between 2040 and 2060, the Southeastern and Southwestern US will become uninhabitable due to temperatures and fires that humans, livestock, and crops cannot endure. Many large cities on the Eastern US seaboard will be underwater. Mass migration to more hospitable places in the US is likely (Xu et al., 2020).

Beyond the inconvenience and expense of floods, fires, and so on, there is an overall stream of consequences leading from carbon to food supply and health:

- Burning of fossil fuels increases CO_2
- Deforestation increases CO_2 in atmosphere
- Greenhouse warming increases
- Earth's temperature increases
- Extreme weather increases
- Ice melting and sea level rise
- Salinization of groundwater and estuaries
- Decrease in freshwater availability
- Ocean acidification affects sea life
- Food supply and health degraded

The threats to life and civilization are very real and possibly devastating.

Stakeholders

Table 3.4 lists classes of **stakeholders** and examples. Expanding a few of these categories of stakeholders, the number of stakeholders becomes substantially larger.

John Browne and Daniel Yergin, in their respective recent books, provide a panoramic view of the energy industry, its evolution, and challenges. They portray a sweeping landscape of stakeholders and vested interests, while also projecting how the ecosystem will eventually move beyond fossil fuels.

Browne is the former CEO of BP and President of the Royal Academy of Engineering. His book (Browne, 2019) provides a

Table 3.4 Stakeholders in Energy and Climate

Stakeholders	Examples
Constituencies	Congress, public
Government agencies	Department of Energy, Environmental Protection Agency, National Oceania and Atmospheric Administration, Federal Emergency Management Agency, states, cities
Agencies workforce	Employees, unions
Industry and institutions	Coal, oil, gas companies and related services, mining companies, renewable energy companies
Industry workforce	Employees, unions
Oversight organizations	Government Accountability Office, Federal Energy Regulatory Commission, International Atomic Energy Agency
Advocacy groups	Intergovernmental Panel on Climate, Change, Environmental Defense Fund, Nature Conservancy, Natural Resources Defense Council, World Wide Fund for Nature, and so on

well-written, easily digestible tour of the history and future of engineering. He uses the terms make, think, connect, build, energize, move, defend, and survive to characterize the contributions of engineering to society. His characterization of the role, history, and future of energy is obviously his strong suit.

Daniel Yergin is a leading authority on energy, geopolitics, and the global economy. A bestselling author and winner of the Pulitzer Prize, he is Vice Chairman of information provider IHS MARKIT. Yergin's book (2020) is profound. When I finished reading it, I felt that I just completed a graduate course on energy, geopolitics, and climate change.

Yergin elaborates "maps" of the economics and politics of energy in the US, Russia, China, the Middle East, and the developing world. Energy has long been central to economic development and, for Russia and the Middle East, dominant in terms of contributions to GDP.

Reductions in the consumption of fossil fuels, particularly dirty fuels like coal, will help the environment but also undermine economies where populations depend on, in effect, energy stipends for their livelihoods. Economic development in poorer countries is likely to depend on dirty, inexpensive, and plentiful fuels—like coal.

Yergin's projections of the likely adoption of renewables, mobility services, and driverless cars are prudent and clearly make the case that a carbon-free future is not just around the corner. The vested interests in the extraction industries and the millions employed in these industries present enormous challenges.

Misinformation and Disinformation

There are almost two billion members of Facebook, Twitter, and so on. They engage in various groups, viewing, posting, liking, retweeting, and so on. Jonathan Haidt, a social psychologist, provides an insightful characterization of the overall phenomenon of social media (Haidt & Rose-Stockwell, 2019; Haidt, 2022). As noted in Chapter 2, he begins by asserting that "human beings evolved to gossip, preen, manipulate, and ostracize." People are now more connected to one another on platforms that magnify these natural tendencies. These platforms, Haidt argues, have been designed to make outrage contagious.

Todd Rose (2022) explores the phenomena of collective illusions. He argues, "Social media platforms allow anyone who's got an axe to grind to pull a digital power play, exerting direct control over the perceived majority and scaring all dissenters into silence with their unfiltered vehemence." He concludes, "Compromising your personal integrity for the sake of belonging quietly wears away at your self-esteem and has been shown to negatively affect personal health in both the short and the long term."

These platforms also enable the "weaponization" of social media (Singer & Brooking, 2018; Zegart, 2022). Adversaries, often via robots, sow mistrust in government and institutions. They attempt to affect elections via misinformation and disinformation. More broadly, they disrupt intelligence gathering and interpretation.

Figure 3.11 provides an overall depiction of the ecosystem of misinformation and disinformation. At the people level, people's communication practices yield views, posts, likes, retweets, and so on. The social media platforms enable instantaneous global broadcasting of this content. Outrageous content flows much faster than tamer communications. Thus, fake news travels much faster than real news.

The social media companies typically earn most of their revenue from advertising, which is typically calculated from page views by users. Their overarching goal, therefore, is to keep people connected. Outrageous content does this better than mundane postings.

The rules of the game at the top of Figure 3.11 have been a work in progress, with one exception. The First Amendment of the US Constitution protects freedom of speech. The US Supreme Court has consistently ruled that lying is protected (Rosenberg, 2021) from criminal prosecution. Civil prosecution is feasible, but can take a long time and be expensive. Deep pockets may bring it back to the Supreme Court for adjudication.

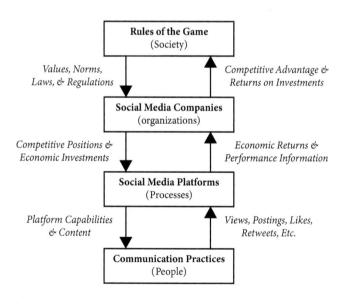

Figure 3.11 Ecosystem of Misinformation and Disinformation

Table 3.5 Stakeholders in Mis/Disinformation

Stakeholders	Examples
Constituencies	Congress, public
Government agencies	Department of Homeland Security, Food and Drug Administration, Intelligence Community, Supreme Court
Agencies workforce	Employees, Unions
Industry and institutions	Social media companies, software platform companies, influencers, advertisers
Industry workforce	Employees, unions
Oversight organizations	Federal Communications Commission, Securities and Exchange Commission, Department of State
Advocacy groups	American Civil Liberties Union, Electronic Frontier Foundation, Institute for Free Speech

While the government cannot ban lying, the social media companies, as private entities, can and do remove content. They can ban users as they have with the former US president. These practices are highly contested, especially by conservatives who see these companies as too liberal. It has recently been argued that these practices will make their way back to the Supreme Court (Barnes & Marimow, 2022).

Table 3.5 lists classes of stakeholders and examples. Expanding a few of these categories of stakeholders, the number and particularly the variety of stakeholders becomes substantially larger. The use of social media is pervasive, not as pervasive as the use of energy, but billions of users means that there is an enormous range of values, concerns, and perceptions of concerning many issues.

Medical Misinformation and Disinformation

Let's look in depth at the public health challenges of medical misinformation and disinformation, which are increasingly pervasive due to numerous online information sources (Rouse, Johns, & Stead, 2022). Of course, people have long spread and believed in rumors, and bought snake oil, health potions, and other shams, so the behavioral and social phenomena are not new. However, the connectivity and speed with which it now happens are unprecedented (Brossard & Scheufele, 2022).

Here are some examples of medical misinformation and disinformation.[1]

- Despite the lack of any evidence that various offerings can boost your immune system, and the possibility of negative side effects, the internet is filled with products that promise such a boost.
- A TV celebrity, an MD, touts unproven weight-loss pills and makes sweeping claims for COVID-19 cures despite minimal or non-existent evidence.
- The prenatal testing industry serves one-third of pregnant women in America, but tests have an 85% false alarm rate, higher for some rare diseases.
- A pregnancy support app includes a section rife with scare stories, conspiracy theories, and outright falsehoods about the safety of vaccines, posted by app users.
- Seven out of eight newly approved drugs that do not provide previously unavailable benefits are promoted as if they do.
- The healthy are harmed due to providers' propensity to advocate what amounts to overdosing, overtreating, and overdiagnosing.
- The American Psychological Association reckons 10,000–20,000 mental-health apps are available for download. But evidence is mounting that privacy risks to users are being ignored. No one is checking if the apps work, either.
- Health insurance offerings that consumers do not realize may not, or will not, pay any claims for reimbursements.

---

[1] See Rouse, Johns, and Stead (2022) for extensive references on the material in this section.

What are the overall health consequences? Falconer (2022) reports on FDA Commissioner Robert Califf's remarks on the impact of medical misinformation and disinformation, "Almost no one in this country should be dying from COVID-19, if we were up to date on our vaccinations and got appropriate anti-viral treatment. But somehow . . . the reliable, truthful messages are not getting across. And it's being washed down by a lot of misinformation, which is leading people to make bad choices that are unfortunate for their health." He argues that decreased life expectancy in the US can be attributed to misinformation and disinformation. If he included opioid overdose deaths due to marketing disinformation regarding oxycontin, Califf's case would be even stronger.

The spectrum of purveyors and consumers of misinformation and disinformation ranges from people who are simply ignorant about science to a radical fringe element who use deliberate mistruths, intimidation, falsified data, and threats of violence in efforts to prevent the use of vaccines and to silence critics. Purveyors tend toward complete mistrust of government and manufacturers, conspiratorial thinking, denialism, low cognitive complexity in thinking patterns, reasoning flaws, and a habit of substituting emotional anecdotes for data.

Consumers of misinformation and disinformation "have been manipulated to think that beliefs needn't change in response to evidence, making us more susceptible to conspiracy theories, science denial, and extremism" (Norman, 2021a). Norman makes a very compelling argument for fostering mental immunity (Norman, 2021b), a possibility I revisit in Chapter 4.

Table 3.6 summarizes the behavioral and social factors underlying consumers' behaviors. These factors represent enormous challenges to remediating the consequences of misinformation and disinformation.

Overarching factors are literacy and numeracy deficits in the US. Over one-fifth of the US population is functionally illiterate; one-third can perform arithmetic, and one in twenty can do algebra (CDC, 2021; NCES, 2022).

Table 3.6 Behavioral and Social Factors
Underlying Misinformation

Factors
Literacy and numeracy deficits
Bounded rationality and satisficing
Heuristics and biases
System 1 dominating System 2
Nudges, for better or worse
Overconfidence and hubris
Motivation
Wishful thinking and reality distortion
Close-minded stance on evidence
Beliefs in contingent truths
Manipulative tendencies
Individual differences
Personality characteristics
Fear, estrangement and resentment
Trust in government and intrapersonal trust
Conflicts of world views
Social and cultural contexts

Matthews and colleagues (2022) argue that:

The interpretation of information relies on human cognitive processes. Cognitive biases or limits in cognitive processing abilities could contribute to differences in the interpretation of facts and data and could make it harder for individuals to differentiate facts from opinions. This, in turn, could contribute to the erosion of trust in institutions that are sources of factual information.

Jacobson, Targonski, and Poland (2007) discuss cognitive and motivational determinants of reasoning flaws in the anti-vaccine movement. Cognitive determinants include desires to find order and predictability in random data, difficulty in detecting and correcting biases in incomplete and unrepresentative data, and eagerness to interpret ambiguous and inconsistent data to fit theories and expectations. Motivational/social determinants include wishful thinking and self-serving distortions of reality, pitfalls of second-hand information, and miscommunication (including mass communication), and exaggerated impressions of social support. Confusion of causation and correlation fits here as well.

Abrams (2021) considers the psychology of why people believe misinformation. There are "five criteria that people use to decide whether information is true: compatibility with other known information, credibility of the source, whether others believe it, whether the information is internally consistent, and whether there is supporting evidence." There are "six degrees of manipulation—impersonation, conspiracy, emotion, polarization, discrediting, and trolling—(that) are used to spread misinformation and disinformation."

"There is often a lot of uncertainty in crisis situations, so people come together and start sharing information in a sort of collective sense-making process. That process can get things right, but it can also get things wrong, producing rumors that turn out to be false."

Psychological research looks at individual differences in demographic, personality, and other traits of those who are more likely to believe misinformation and conspiracy theories, with the ultimate goal of characterizing the underlying processes that lead people to accept such claims.

Psychological research backs several methods of countering misinformation. One is to debunk incorrect information after it has spread. Much more effective, though, is inoculating people against fake news before they're exposed—a strategy known as "prebunking." I return to this in Chapter 4.

Once people have processed information that seems vaguely credible to them, it is just not possible to take it back. Retractions of misinformation are notoriously ineffective. We do need to acknowledge that strong believers will not be persuaded even with hard evidence. So it's always best to target the undecided majority.

Cultural and social context can significantly affect perceptions and reactions to misinformation and disinformation. Del Real

(2021) reports lessons from a year covering conspiracy theories. He observes that "the truth is not something merely to be found and disclosed, but rather that, in the broader sense, it is something that is negotiated." He argues that, "The search for truth is also messier than it used to be now that everyone has a video production studio in their pockets." He concludes that, "The Internet has not only made it easier for conspiratorial communities to organize, but it has also made conspiracy mongering substantially less arduous."

We need to understand the cultural currents leading to people's perceptions of conspiracies, including human emotions—fear, estrangement, resentment—that underlie them. Confirmation bias and the illusory truth effects are among two of the relevant cognitive biases. It should be recognized that people learn most of their beliefs from other people—teachers, colleagues, friends, and family.

An overarching and pervasive issue is trust. Americans' trust in government has fallen from 80% in the 1960s to 20% today (Pew, 2021; Taylor, 2022). One consequence has been far higher levels of death due to the Omicron variant of the coronavirus compared to other OECD countries due to much lower population vaccination rates in the US than in these other countries. Trust in government and interpersonal trust, in conjunction with extensive disinformation, are likely underlying causes (Lancet, 2022; Mueller & Lutz, 2022).

Interactions among Challenges

There are strong interactions among these four ecosystems as shown in Figure 3.12. Educated people tend to be healthier. Inequalities in access to care often undermine health. Consequences of climate change will inordinately affect the uneducated and unhealthy. Misinformation and disinformation are pervasive, and exacerbate the other three challenges. The interactions among these phenomena are important, as a whack-a-mole approach to each challenge will be costly and unproductive. A more integrated approach is needed,

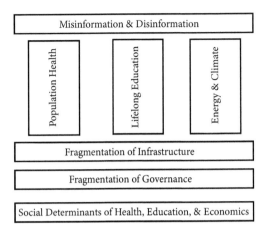

Figure 3.12   Context of Four Challenges

an approach embodied by understanding and thought, more than slogans and pundits' proclamations.

Consider the interactions in Figure 3.12. Misinformation and disinformation poses enormous public health risks (Rouse, Johns, & Stead, 2022). Misleading advertisements (e.g., oxycontin), and misinformed or deceptive media pundits cause people to adopt practices to their detriment, or perhaps death. Such misinformation and disinformation is protected by free speech rights.

Education can provide the means to deter and mitigate misinformation and disinformation. As I later elaborate, it has been shown that students can learn how to detect, diagnose, and remediate false claims. There are compelling and viable proposals for how best to foster mental immunity to misinformation and disinformation (Norman, 2021b).

People's orientation toward energy and climate, and associated behaviors, are strongly affected by misinformation and disinformation. Vested interests in the fossil-based energy industries, as well as politicians that depend on campaign contributions for these industries, do their best to mislead the overall population (Yergin, 2020). As a result, people are skeptical of claims about the impact of carbon emissions on global warming.

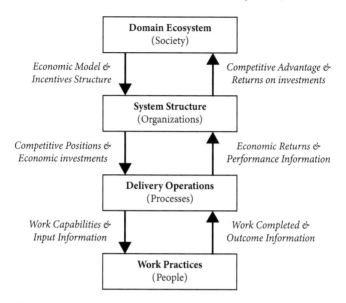

Figure 3.13 Generalized Multi-Level Framework

Figure 3.13 represents a generalized version of Figures 3.2, 3.5, 3.9, and 3.11. To compare our four challenges, we need to address the phenomena occurring at the various levels of the system. Table 3.7 summarizes the phenomena and driving forces at each level of the challenges.

Figure 3.14 illustrates how the challenges influence each other, both negatively and positively. For example, health and education interact to undermine or reinforce each other. Misinformation and disinformation undermine health, education, and energy initiatives.

Note that the upper left block indicates "affects," while all the other blocks indicate "improves." This reflects the reality that information can improve or degrade awareness, knowledge, polarization, and trust. In this way, the mis/disinformation challenge is a threat to successfully addressing the other three challenges. Consequently, we need means to mitigate this threat. I discuss how we might do this in Chapter 4.

Table 3.7 Phenomena and Driving Forces for Each Challenge

Level	Challenge			
	Population Health	Lifelong Education	Energy and Climate	Mis/Dis Information
Society	Values, norms, incentives, rules, regulations	Values, norms, incentives, rules, regulations	Values, norms, incentives, rules, regulations	Values, norms, incentives, rules, regulations
Driving Forces	Health challenges availability, costs	Workforce needs, content, costs	Environmental threats, costs	Free speech, liabilities, costs
Organizations	Providers, payers, pharma, device cos, licensing and accreditation	Public school boards, administrators, unions	Public utility comms, energy companies, utilities	Public oversight orgs, social media companies, advertisers
Driving Forces	Reputation, revenue, profits	Reputation, budget, salaries	Reputation, revenue, profits	Reputation, revenue, profits
Processes	Care capacities and consumables, health information	Educational programs and technologies	Service stations, utility services, supply chains	Posting, liking, retweeting, recommending
Driving Forces	Demands, costs, reimbursements, technologies	Community content priorities, enrollment, costs	Demands, costs, profits, regulations	No. of members, active users, no. of advertisers
People	Patients, families, and clinicians	Students, families, and teachers	Consumers of energy	Consumers of information
Driving Forces	Lifestyle, environment, genetics, healthcare	Family, environment, experiences, aptitudes	Availability, reliability, price, affordability, envir. awareness	Availability, reliability, interests, affiliations

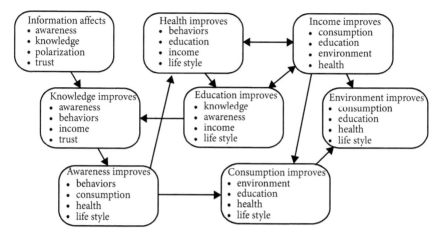

Figure 3.14 Interactions Among Challenges

Conclusions

In this chapter, I have provided a deeper exploration of the four societal challenges. They are laced with various idiosyncrasies associated with health, education, energy, and so on. However, as I later elaborate in more detail, the overall approach I am advocating involves seeing these challenges as parts of a whole societal picture.

In particular, it is important that we return to the notion of fragmented systems. Information sharing and service coordination suffer from pervasive fragmentation in the US. This is true of healthcare (Rouse, Johns, & Pepe, 2017, 2019), education (Rouse, 2016), and energy and climate (Yergin, 2020).

Mitigating the infodemic of medical misinformation and disinformation (Rouse, Johns, & Stead, 2022) is made more difficult by organizational fragmentation, as is addressing the weaponization of social media (Singer & Brooking, 2018; Zegart, 2022). The fragmentation of government in general (Khanna, 2022) pervasively exacerbates everything.

Nevertheless, we begin in Chapter 4 to map out an approach to overcoming fragmentation. It involves a long-term, multi-stage process where successive improvements are sequentially staged, deployed, and evaluated. Lessons learned from deployment experiences and evaluation findings are systematically employed to refine or perhaps rethink subsequent stages.

References

Abrams, Z. (2021). Controlling the spread of misinformation: Psychologists' research on misinformation may help in the fight to debunk myths surrounding COVID-19. *APA Monitor*, 52 (2), https://www.apa.org/monitor/2021/03/controlling-misinformation

Barnes, R., & Marimow, A.E. (2022). A landmark Supreme Court fight over social media now looks likely. *Washington Post*, September 19.

Brossard, D., & Scheufele, D.A. (2022). The chronic growing pains of communicating science online. *Science*, 375 (6581), 613–614.

Browne, J. (2019). *Make, Think, Imagine: Engineering the Future of Civilization*. New York: Pegasus Books.

CDC (2021). *Understanding Literacy & Numeracy in the US*. Atlanta, GA: Centers for Disease Control and Prevention.

Del Real, J.A. (2021). An American Tradition: Lessons from a year covering conspiracy theories. *Washington Post*. December 30.

Falconer, R. (2022). Misinformation spurring US life expectancy "erosion" FDA chief says. *Axios*, May 8.

Haidt, J. (2022). Why the past 10 years of American life have been uniquely stupid: It's not just a phase. *The Atlantic*, April.

Haidt, J.R., & Rose-Stockwell, T. (2019). The dark psychology of social networks: Why it feels like everything has gone haywire. *The Atlantic*, December.

Jacobson, R.M., Targonski, P.V., & Poland, G.A. (2007). A taxonomy of reasoning flaws in the anti-vaccine movement. *Vaccine*, 25, 3146–3152.

Khanna, R. (2022). *Dignity in a Digital Age: Making Tech Work for All of Us*. New York: Simon & Schuster.

Lancet (2022). Pandemic preparedness and COVID-19: an exploratory analysis of infection and fatality rates, and contextual factors associated with preparedness in 177 countries, from Jan 1, 2020, to Sept 30,

2021, *Lancet*, COVID-19 National Preparedness Collaborators, February 1, 2022, https://doi.org/10.1016/S0140–6736(22)00172–6.

Matthews, L.J., Parker, A.M., Carman, K.G., Kerber, R., & Kavanagh, J. (2022). *Individual Differences in Resistance to Truth Decay: Exploring the Role of Reasoning and Cognitive Biases*. Santa Monica, CA: RAND Corporation.

Mueller, B., & Lutz, E. (2022). US has far higher covid death rate than other wealthy countries, *New York Times*, February 1.

NCES (2022). *Literacy and Numeracy Skills of U.S. Men and Women*, https://nces.ed.gov/pubs2018/2018164/index.asp.

Norman, A. (2021a). The cause of America's post-truth predicament. *Scientific American*, May 18.

Norman, A. (2021b). *Mental Immunity: Infectious Ideas, Mind-Parasites, and the Search for a Better Way to Think*. New York: Harper.

NWS (2020). *Climate Versus Weather*, https://www.weather.gov/climateservices/CvW, Accessed 11-16-20.

Pew (2021). *Public Trust in Government: 1958–2021*. Washington, DC: Pew Research Center.

Rose, T. (2022). *Collective Illusions: Conformity, Complicity, and the Science of Why We Make Bad Decisions*. New York: Hachette.

Rosenberg, I. (2021). *The Fight for Free Speech: Ten Cases that Define Our First Amendment Freedoms*. New York: New York University Press.

Rouse, W.B. (2014). Earth as a system. In M. Mellody, Ed., *Can Earth's and Society's Systems Meet the Needs of 10 Billion People?* (pp. 20–23). Washington, DC: National Academies Press.

Rouse, W.B. (2016). *Universities as Complex Enterprises: How Academia Works, Why It Works These Ways, and Where the University Enterprise Is Headed*. New York: Wiley.

Rouse, W.B., & Cortese, D.A. (Eds.) (2010). *Engineering the System of Healthcare Delivery*. Amsterdam: IOS Press.

Rouse, W.B., Johns, M.M.E., & Pepe, K.M. (2017). Learning in the healthcare enterprise. *Journal of Learning Health Systems*, 1 (4), https://doi.org/10.1002/lrh2.10024.

Rouse, W.B., Johns, M.M.E., & Pepe, K.M. (2019). Service supply chains for population health: Overcoming fragmentation of service delivery ecosystems. *Journal of Learning Health Systems*, 3 (2), https://doi.org/10.1002/lrh2.10186.

Rouse, W.B., Johns, M.M.E., & Stead, W.W. (2022). *Medical Misinformation & Disinformation*. Washington, DC: McCourt School of Public Policy, Georgetown University.

Rouse, W.B., Lombardi, J.V., & Craig, D.D. (2018). Modeling research universities: Predicting probable futures of public vs. private and large vs. small research universities. *Proceedings of the National Academy of Sciences*, 115 (50), 12582–12589.

Rouse, W.B., & Serban, N. (2014). *Understanding and Managing the Complexity of Healthcare*. Cambridge, MA: MIT Press.

Singer, P.W., & Brooking, E.T. (2018). *Like War: The Weaponization of Social Media*. Boston: Houghton Mifflin.

Taylor, A. (2022). Researchers are asking why some countries were better prepared for covid. One surprisingly answer: trust. *Washington Post*, February 1.

Xu, C., Kohler, T.A., Lenton, T.M., Svenning, J-C., & Scheffer, M. (2020). Future of the human climate niche. *Proceedings of the National Academies of Sciences*, 117 (21), 11350–11355.

Yergin, D. (2020). *The New Map: Energy, Climate, and the Clash of Nations*. New York: Penguin Press.

Yu, Z., Rouse, W.B., Serban, N., & Veral, E. (2016). A data-rich agent-based decision support model for hospital consolidation. *Journal of Enterprise Transformation*, 6 (3/4), 136–161.

Zegart, A.B. (2022). *Spies, Lies & Algorithms: The History and Future of American Intelligence*. Princeton, NJ: Princeton University Press.

4

Translating Insights into Action Plans

Understanding, Gaining, and Sustaining Stakeholders' Support

Introduction

We need to translate the findings from earlier chapters into alternative courses of action, as well as formulate explanations of findings and possible ways forward in stakeholder-friendly terms. Acting in transparent ways that stakeholders can understand and evaluate is central to stakeholders trusting change.

Table 4.1 illustrates how understanding translates into courses of action over time, namely years and decades. In this chapter, I discuss these potential aspirational courses of action in considerable detail. Chapter 5 addresses how stakeholders will be supported to understand and trust these alternative ways forward for each challenge.

I hasten to emphasize that the actions summarized in Table 4.1 are not quick fixes. I expect that achieving ultimate success will take at least a decade for all four challenges. We need to formulate a vision, articulate it to all stakeholders, provide the necessary resources, and rigorously execute it. This will enable attracting, engaging, inspiring, recruiting, and retaining stakeholder support.

Beyond Quick Fixes. William B. Rouse, Oxford University Press. © William B. Rouse (2023).
DOI: 10.1093/oso/9780198892533.003.0004

Table 4.1 Insights into Action Plans

Aspirations	Challenges			
	Population Health	Lifelong Education	Energy and Climate	Mis/Disinformation
Starting point (status quo)	High costs and poor outcomes	High costs and poor outcomes	Unacceptable emission levels	Chaos and confusion
Baseline initial success	Information sharing	National graduation standards	Emission limitations	Social media limitations
Leveraging baseline	Care coordination across services	National curriculum standards for STEM and STW	Renewables, including nuclear	Free speech with responsibility
Innovative leaps	Single payer	Elimination of reliance on property taxes	Storage and transmission innovations	Education on information management
Ultimate success	Integrated delivery system	Integrated delivery system	Green energy workforce	Pervasive mental immunity

Implications

Some readers, particularly in the US, may disagree with the aspirations represented in Table 4.1. They are likely to presume that the level of integration envisioned can only be accomplished by federal government control of everything, as is common in many OECD countries. However, as illustrated by the example "positive deviants" discussed later in this chapter, the private sector can play a dominant role in delivering services. The federal government can facilitate the setting of standards and provide some of the needed financial resources.

As Scott (1998) argues, government has often been inept in state-initiated social engineering. He asserts that there are four elements associated with such failures:

- Attempts to administratively reorder society
- A modernist ideology, relying solely on science and technology
- An authoritarian state
- A prostrate civil society

He might characterize this book as reflecting a modernist ideology, but the other three elements are absent from my treatise.

Of course, some readers who are aligned with Hayek and Friedman (see Chapter 2) may feel that integration will undermine the freedoms of the marketplace, limiting competition and profit making. They might argue that profiteering, depressions and recessions, unemployment, and public health crises are simply the prices we pay for freedom. From this perspective, being the highest OECD spenders in healthcare and education, and the poorest performers, assures that some stakeholders are seeing great financial returns.

This book is in complete conflict with this perspective. In contrast, the overarching objective of the line of reasoning articulated here is the assurance of a healthy, educated, and productive population that is competitive in the global population. Quite simply, the goal is for everyone to succeed. All stakeholders—public and private—need to work together to make this happen.

Finally, it is important to relate the goals in Table 4.1 to the United Nations Strategic Development Goals (UN, 2023). All of these seventeen goals are aligned with the goals just outlined. Most are closely aligned, while a few are at least philosophically aligned. For example, gender equality (5), reduced inequalities (10), and peace, justice, and strong institutions (16) do not explicitly appear in Table 4.1 but are compatible. Discussion in Chapter 7 portrays this philosophical alignment in more depth.

Population Health

As just noted, the US has the highest per capita costs of healthcare, compared with other OECD countries. We have among the poorest outcomes compared to these countries. This is due, in part, to making much smaller investments in social services. Further, the medical services offered are quite fragmented, as outlined in Chapter 3.

The first step to changing this situation is information sharing. The 21st Century Cures Act requires healthcare providers to give patients access to all of the health information in their electronic medical records "without delay" and without charge. This is a great first step. We need all providers, including those providing social services, to have access to patients' complete health and well-being records.

Assume a patient's primary care physician (PCP) uses Cerner's electronic health record (EHR) while the hospital where the patient recently underwent a procedure uses Epic's EHR, and the patient accesses public social services via his or her city. All of the information generated in the course of using these services should be available to the patient and the providers via a single integrated portal.

Once this baseline is achieved, the next step is care coordination across all population health services. The PCP should interact with the hospital's specialists, and perhaps be aware that the patient experienced a period of homelessness a few years ago, but recently earned an associate's degree at the local community college and now has a much better job. The portal just mentioned would provide the functionality to help with this coordination.

The overall system needs to evolve toward single-payer. Employer-based health insurance has depressed wages as providers charge patients with such insurance more than, for example, Medicare patients. This hidden tax is unfair to these people. Single-payer does not imply the government takes over healthcare. Unified payments are the key. Kaiser Permanente, which I will discuss in a later section, is a great example of private-sector innovation.

The eventual outcome is an integrated delivery system with, for example, the whole population health system using Kaiser Permanente's business model. There may be many companies involved, as well as government involvement at the local, state, and federal levels. However, from the perspective of patients, their families, and frontline clinicians, the delivery system would seem to be one integrated system. These stakeholders are much more interested in high-quality, affordable services, rather than who owns what.

In a recent piece (Rouse, Johns, & Curran, 2024), we outline population health in terms of human well-being. Our overall line of reasoning is summarized in Figure 4.1. Note that the bulleted lists below each topic are intended to be illustrative, not exhaustive, of the issues discussed in the full book chapter.

We begin with definitions of well-being, then consider the behavioral and social phenomena that must be addressed. We next address the performance challenges faced in the US when trying to assure well-being. We need a national well-being system. Unfortunately, the inherent complexity of the highly fragmented US system seems to preclude the requisite information sharing and care coordination across the stakeholder organizations in the federation that is misnamed as a system.

I am not suggesting an integrated government-run system. Recent experiences (Economist, 2023: WSJ, 2023) suggest that health systems operated by governments are by no means panaceas. The government's role envisioned here includes regulations, standards, and perhaps financial incentives. The private sector can focus on providing efficient and effective services, with frequent innovations due to competitive pressures. The later example of Kaiser Permanente provides a compelling illustration.

We review a range of interventions, as shown in Figure 4.1. We discuss the role of digital technologies in enabling these interventions. The promise and risks of these technologies are summarized. We next articulate how to gain the upsides and avoid the downsides to assure human well-being in a digital age. Finally, we outline the management implications of pursuing our recommendations.

It is clear that we know how to conceptualize and address human well-being. However, along with all of the challenges considered in this book, we have difficulty mustering the will, commitment, and resources to plan and act to achieve these ends. I consider this dilemma in depth in Chapter 5.

Lifelong Education

The US has among the highest per-student costs of education, compared to other OECD countries. We have among the poorest educational outcomes compared to these countries. This is due to enormous variability in K-12, which is controlled by 14,000 independent school boards and relies on property tax revenues to provide the lion's share of school budgets. The value of the housing being taxed has a huge impact on what resources are available.

Each school board decides on the K-12 curriculum, how it is delivered, and associated budgets. There is great pressure to promote and graduate every student. However, what does a high school diploma imply? What can employers and colleges expect from these graduates?

The first step toward lifelong education should be national standards for high school graduation, perhaps assessed by externally managed testing services. This is the way Advanced Placement course exams are managed. Mathews (2021) discusses this at length.

The next step is national curriculum standards. This is particularly important for students aspiring to pursue STEM (science, technology, engineering, and mathematics) majors in college. This would

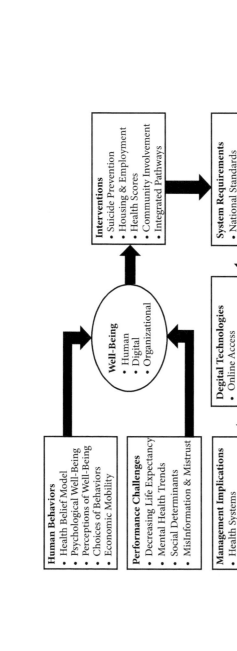

Figure 4.1 Line of Reasoning for Well-Being

also benefit those entering the "skilled technical workforce" (STW) via integrated high school and community college programs. Such programs lead to well-paying jobs that require technical knowledge and skills but not a Bachelor of Science (BS) degree. These jobs often pay double what a freshly minted non-STEM college graduate earns.

The elimination of reliance on property taxes would enable meeting the graduation and curriculum standards. A mix of state and federal monies could fund this, as done in other countries. Tax revenues, as always, would provide the funds, but the taxation mechanisms would likely differ substantially.

The eventual outcome is an integrated education delivery system. All high school students would meet the same criteria, enabled by fully funded programs. These programs would differ for STEM, the arts, and the skilled technical workforce, but all would produce graduates capable of successfully moving to the next stage of their careers.

Speaking of careers, the integrated education delivery system also needs to provide ongoing education for those well along in their careers, including those who seek to change career paths. High-quality online programs may fill this need, as excellent offerings have emerged in recent years. An example of this type of education is discussed in the next section.

Figure 4.2 summarizes the post-secondary education pipeline in the US (Verma et al., 2022). Two transition probabilities most affect the STEM talent flow: the probability that a K-12 student graduates "STEM ready," P_{SR}, and the probability that a college student enrolled in a STEM major graduates with a STEM degree, P_{SG}. In the US, these probabilities are 0.16 and 0.50, respectively. Thus, only 8% of K-12 students enter the STEM-related workforce.

The performance of the K-12 ecosystem in the US severely undermines the talent pipeline. A significant portion of K-12 schools does not even offer the courses needed to become STEM-ready. The opportunity for a high-quality K-12 education is most affected by ZIP code rather than student aptitude due to local school budgets being based on local property taxes—the more valuable the homes, the more money for schools.

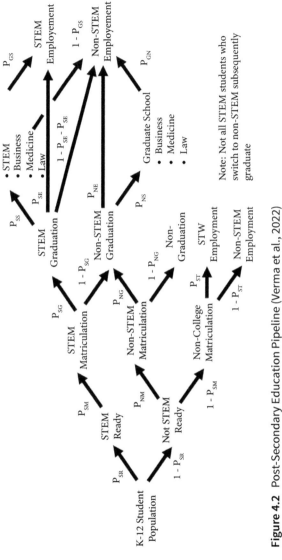

Figure 4.2 Post-Secondary Education Pipeline (Verma et al., 2022)

There is also a substantial lack of K-12 outcome data. As noted above, there are no national standards for high school graduation and no standards for curricula, as they are controlled by 14,000 local school boards. These boards tend to focus on maximizing the percentage of students that graduate rather than assessing the knowledge and skills of graduates. Social promotion can predominate, which is the practice of promoting students to the next grade level despite not having learned the material they were taught or having achieved expected learning standards.

Energy and Climate

Unacceptable emission levels of carbon and methane have led to global warming, causing storms, floods, fires, and sea level rise. There seems to be general, but not universal, agreement that rebuilding after each disaster is an expensive and inadequate strategy.

The first step is emission limitations. We have made notable progress in this area, despite often fierce resistance from major emitting enterprises. We need to accelerate the movement to renewable energy sources—water, wind, and solar—as well as next-generation nuclear. The costs of renewable energy have dramatically decreased in recent years.

We need to invest in creating and deploying energy storage and transmission innovations. The wind does not always blow, and the sun does not always shine. We need to store the energy created by these sources to be able to access it when needed. Investment in transmission infrastructure is needed as the sources of renewable energy are not always near where the energy is needed. While we can build a traditional electric power generation facility anywhere, wind and solar do not allow this discretion.

The existing fossil energy workforce needs to be transformed into a green energy workforce. The opportunity is there—the Bureau of Labor Statistics reports that two of the fastest-growing jobs are solar panel installer and wind turbine maintainer. We need to invest in the education of this workforce, perhaps using the high-quality online courses discussed earlier. This approach could enable workers to more quickly transition to the hands-on training that is inherently needed in this domain.

Figure 4.3 provides an overview of the US electric grid (NREL, 2010). Of particular interest is the portion of the figure labeled Generation. Solar and wind sources are depicted, as is conventional centralized generation, typically fueled by coal, gas, or nuclear. As we move from the latter to the former, the energy industry is changing.

Employment is 7.8 million jobs in the energy sector, growing by 4% annually (DOE, 2022). Around 40% of jobs are in "net-zero emissions" occupations. There are 2.6 million jobs in the motor vehicle and components portion of this sector, increasing by 9.8% annually. The largest percent increases are in electric vehicles (EVs) and

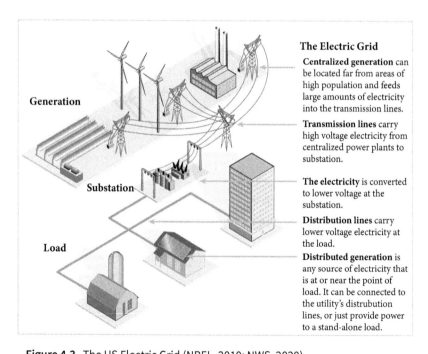

Figure 4.3 The US Electric Grid (NREL, 2010; NWS, 2020)

Climate Versus Weather. https://www.weather.gov/climateservices/CvW, Accessed 11-16-20.

hybrids. There are 908,000 jobs in energy supply portion of this sector, down 3.1% annually; the largest decreases are 6.4% in petroleum and 11.8% in coal.

Thus, the transition to green employment has started. A great example is in Scotland, where wind jobs associated with an ocean-based wind farm of eighty-four turbines provide more than 10% of Britain's electricity, and more than 50% on gusty days. This has created over 31,000 jobs (Reed, 2022). As more of the electricity in Figure 4.3 is generated by renewables, the environmental benefits of battery electric vehicles (BEVs) are much greater. Recharging BEVs with electricity from coal-fired plants completely undermines such benefits (Liu, Rouse, & Hanawalt, 2018).

There are, nevertheless, hurdles affecting the energy transition (Gillis & Norris, 2022). There are significant grid capacity issues causing "huge backlogs of renewable energy projects have built up around the world as developers are refused permission to pump their power into the grid. In Germany, for instance, delays in grid development have prevented wind farms in the north from powering the industrial south." An overarching issue is who pays for grid upgrades (i.e., utilities vs. public vs. providers of renewable energy).

Misinformation and Disinformation

This challenge prompted me to title the first chapter in this book chaos and confusion. Not only has this infodemic unsettled politics and other areas. It has actually exacerbated the other three challenges. People do not know what to believe and who to trust regarding health, education, and energy.

The first step in addressing this challenge is understanding what social media limitations are needed. This is very controversial. The social media platforms are all privately owned. Thus, similar to other media, they have the right to publish or not publish whatever content they choose. This tends to discriminate against hate speech, for example.

However, a recent ***Washington Post*** article reported on efforts to get the Supreme Court to require social media to publish everything (Barnes & Marimow, 2022). These companies do not want to sell advertisements to customers that may appear next to hateful postings. Would Proctor & Gamble want advertisements for Pampers to appear on the same screen posting advocating genocide? This ongoing debate is unlikely to be settled quickly.

We need to get to the point that free speech is protected but people are responsible for what they say. The Supreme Court has repeatedly ruled that lying is completely legal. If the advertisement leads people to die (e.g., oxycontin overdoses), the legal system eventually catches up with the culprits, but almost one million people have thus far died. Responsibility for the consequences of lying should take much less than 10–20 years.

The key is education on information management. Students are now being taught how to determine if information, perhaps unintentionally, is wrong and, especially, if it is an outright lie. A few experiments have shown that this works (Poland & Jacobson, 2011; Chou, Oh, & Klein, 2018; Trethewey, 2020; Murthy, 2021; Wineburg et al., 2022). We need to scale up such programs for all students and all people. We need a much more savvy population when it comes to misinformation and disinformation.

We ultimately need pervasive mental immunity (Norman, 2021). There are well-thought-out approaches to this, with positive evaluations emerging. Norman argues that "A belief is reasonable if it can withstand the challenges to it that genuinely arise." An interesting issue is whether the claimant bears the burden of proof or the challenger bears the burden of disproof.

Overall, we need to evolve into a culture that finds lying unacceptable. Let the liars beware that they will be shunned, perhaps even prosecuted. For example, companies with misleading ads about the effectiveness of their drugs will experience dramatic reductions in sales for all their products. Consequences that are socially enforced may be more effective than legal consequences.

Who should be the actors enabling mis/disinterventions? Figure 4.4 provides an initial mapping from actors to interventions

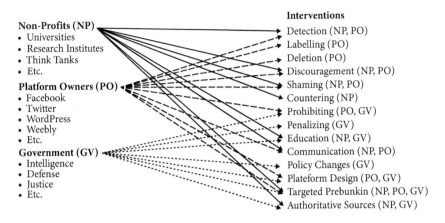

Figure 4.4 Interventions and Agents to Counter Mis/Dis (Rouse, Johns, & Stead, 2022)

(Rouse, Johns, & Stead, 2022). This portrays who **could** intervene, but we need to understand who **would** intervene. There appear to be four criteria:

- Who has the expertise to exercise the intervention?
- Who has the human and financial resources to support the intervention?
- Who has the legal authority to perform the interventions?
- Given all of the above, who has the motivation to act?

I expect that the answers to these questions will depend on the context. Medical misinformation and disinformation might prompt different responses than those for retail or election domains in terms of who is affected, what consequences are likely, and what mitigations are possible.

Leveraging Positive Deviants

Why should we believe that the aspirations elaborated in Table 4.1 are achievable? Are there any examples of success in pursuing such multi-stage plans? What can we learn from these examples?

In every domain, there are people or organizations whose uncommon behaviors and strategies enable them to formulate and implement better solutions to problems than their peers, while having access to the same resources and facing similar or worse challenges. Such people or organizations are termed positive deviants.

In this section, I discuss compelling examples for each of the four challenges. We have experienced success in pursuing aspirations, as summarized in Table 4.1. It is quite useful to learn why and how these successes resulted.

Health—Kaiser Permanente

My research into healthcare delivery has involved working with over ten major providers, involving several well-known thought leaders, many of whom are members of the National Academy of Medicine. Several books have resulted (Rouse, 2010; Rouse & Cortese, 2010; Rouse & Serban, 2014).

I have, of course, experienced being a patient of several providers and being insured by several payers. I became a member of Kaiser Permanente (KP) in 2017 when I moved to Washington, DC. I encountered a complete outlier, very much a positive deviant in terms of accessibility and quality of service.

KP was founded in 1945 by industrialist Henry J. Kaiser and physician Sidney Garfield in Oakland, CA. Operating in eight states and Washington, DC, it serves over 12 million members. KP operates thirty-nine hospitals and more than 700 medical offices, with over 300,000 personnel, including more than 87,000 physicians and nurses.

KP represents what population health should be, as summarized in Table 4.1 (McKinsey, 2009; Pines et al., 2015). While KP does not yet integrate educational and social services, it is easy to imagine its business model adapting to such needs.

KP closely coordinates primary, secondary, and hospital care, with a strong emphasis on prevention. They extensively use care pathways and electronic medical records. They carefully coordinate the work done by primary care physicians, specialists, hospitals, pharmacies, laboratories, and others. This improves care quality, makes care delivery more convenient for members, and increases communication among all the people providing care. It also enables them to find efficiencies that reduce costs, improve or maintain quality, and allow for innovation. KP's goal is to improve the overall health of the community, one person at a time (McKinsey, 2009).

KP is an integrated system consisting of three distinctly separate, but related entities: a health plan that bears insurance risk, medical groups of physicians, and a hospital system. The financial incentive is to provide high-quality, affordable care, and manage population health rather than generating a high volume of compensable services. Both the health plan and the medical group are aligned and accountable for a global budget, and only contract directly with one another for the provision of medical services. All three entities share in the goal, reflected in the organization's capitated payment system, of keeping patients healthy while optimizing utilization (Pines et al., 2015)

How does a KP member experience this? As KP is the provider, payer, and pharmacy, I only need one relationship to cover my complete health needs. They are responsible for these needs within the capitated payments of Medicare Advantage. Consequently, KP makes more profit when I am healthy. They do their best to keep me healthy with emails, surveys (e.g., on mental health), and other forms of outreach. Other than my monthly Medicare deduction from my Social Security benefit, I spend very little on healthcare.

I see the population health column of Table 4.1, resulting in Medicare Advantage for everyone as provided by KP. I imagine there will be multiple private sector participants in this integrated system, some of them profit-making. However, as a member, I will not have to know about any of the pieces. I will just experience high-quality, affordable, and fully understandable care.

How will this happen and what will it cost? I address the integration of how we can address the challenges in Chapter 5 and the economics of the portfolio of endeavors in Chapter 6.

Education—BASIS and Individuals with Disabilities Education Act (IDEA)

The notion of charter schools emerged in the 1970s and state legislation began in the 1990s. Charter schools receive government funding but operate independently of the established state school system in which it is located. It operates according to the basic principle of autonomy for accountability. It is freed from typical local rules but is accountable for educational results. There are 3.4 million students enrolled in over 7,500 charter schools across the US (Mathews, 2021).

The KIPP Academy (Knowledge Is Power Program) was founded in 1994 and currently enrolls 120,000 students in 280 schools in the US. KIPP is a network of free, open-enrollment college-preparatory schools in low-income communities. It is the largest charter school network in the US. Its approach is quite different from BASIS or IDEA, as discussed next.

The first BASIS Curriculum School was founded in Tucson in 1998, with the goal of educating students at an internationally competitive level. They currently enroll 19,400 students in twenty-eight schools in the US. IDEA was founded in 2000 and currently enrolls 80,000 students in 143 schools. Its mission is to serve impoverished students.

The BASIS and IDEA curricula are built around Advanced Placement (AP) courses. The pilot program for AP exams was launched in 1952 and tested high schoolers in eleven subjects. In 1954, around 530 high school students took AP exams. The AP program began in 1955, inspired by a fear that American high-school students were falling behind the rest of the world, the Soviet Union in particular. The number of AP exams taken in May 1998 surpassed 1 million for the first time and in May 2018, the number (was) expected to surpass 5 million. AP tests, which are written and graded by outside experts, cannot be dumbed down by schools.

The BASIS and IDEA programs are tough. That is what makes them intriguing. Even the most ambitious schools in low-income areas usually try to get no higher than grade level. IDEA aims far above that. Every student must take eleven AP courses and tests to graduate. BASIS and IDEA fill eight of the top ten slots in The Washington Post's list of America's Most Challenging High Schools (Mathews, 2017).

> The average AP test passing rate of the three BASIS schools in the top 10 is 84 percent. The average for the five IDEA schools in the top 10 is 21.4 percent. But the BASIS schools in Arizona average only 5 percent impoverished students per school. The portion of children from low-income families in IDEA schools is usually 80 percent or more. (Research points to significant academic benefits for AP students even if they fail the exams.) (Mathews, 2017)

Not surprisingly, success requires enormous effort by students (e.g., homework, longer hours, AP courses, and exams), extraordinarily committed educators, ranging from leaders to administrators to teachers, and committed parent involvement. Nevertheless, these positive deviants show that enormous success is definitely feasible, including for children from low-income families.

Energy—Community Examples

Positive deviance examples can be drawn from a variety of communities. In this section, I discuss examples of community energy transition in South Asia and behavioral changes among institutional investors. I chose these examples to illustrate the range of stakeholders in addressing this challenge.

Herington (2018) studied energy access transitions in South Asia in terms of positive deviance and enabling mechanisms for social change at the community level. He was concerned with where positive, norm-defying change has occurred within collective energy transitions at the community scale in rural India and Nepal. He presents three case studies:

- India: adoption of new cooking practices, not using wood for fuel
- India: adoption of cleaner cooking fuels
- Nepal: post-earthquake recovery and reconstruction of local hydropower energy infrastructure, replacing backup diesel generators and kerosene lamps

His findings identify motivation (both intrinsic and extrinsic forms), practice leadership, and trust between stakeholders as critical mechanisms that support social transformations away from traditional, normative practices, and toward modern clean energy transitions. More specifically, his findings include several themes:

- Collective motivation: push versus pull levers for motivating a shift in energy practices.
- Practice leadership: the pivotal role of agency in energy transitions.
- Trust: establishing coalitions for transformations in practice.
- Adaptive management: learning by doing and responding to change and uncertainty.
- Transition resilience: managing disruptions.

Walton (2018) addresses a very different community. Her research was designed to deepen understanding of institutional fossil fuel divestment, as one approach to addressing climate change:

Since 2011, a growing global social movement has emerged focused on divestment of fossil fuel company holdings and reinvestment of those resources in clean energy. Investors have conventionally relied on fossil fuel holdings as investment portfolio mainstays. Therefore, leaders' divestment behavior constituted positive deviance: intentionally engaging in non-normative behavior intended to contribute to successful outcomes. Findings included that leaders engaging in divestment may experience higher levels of satisfaction, pride, happiness, and engagement with organizational roles. Results yielded insights into organizational leadership, climate action, and utility of positive deviance. (Walton, 2018)

These two examples, from quite different domains, illustrate common findings. Stakeholder agency, motivation, and leadership were central to a willingness to engage in positive deviance. We will need to leverage these factors in our strategy for moving forward, which I discuss in Chapter 7.

Mis/Dis—Public Health Smoking Campaign

If we characterize misinformation and disinformation as a public health challenge, then an obvious public health positive deviant is the success of the antismoking campaign in the US (Polyakova & Gonzalez, 2018).

The effort to reduce smoking in the United States began in 1964, when the government acknowledged for the first time that smoking is harmful to health. By 2015, the United States had managed to cut the smoking rate by more than half. When the campaign began, doctors were still telling pregnant women that it was safe for them to smoke. Fifty years later, smoking has been banned in many public spaces.

What made this campaign so successful? First, the government used its regulatory powers. Much like Big Tobacco in the 1950s, the tech industry today operates in an unregulated environment. Facebook, Twitter, and Google are all keen to avoid being treated as media companies, which would make them subject to a slew of Federal Communications Commission (FCC) regulations.

So far, when left to their own devices, the companies have made only superficial changes to their platforms at the behest of new European regulations around user data privacy. These voluntary efforts are failing to curtail the spread of disinformation, and sooner or later the tech industry will have to face the same FCC restrictions on content and advertising as traditional media—which would undoubtedly help to reduce the spread of erroneous reporting.

Second, the messenger matters. The Office of the US Surgeon General, which published a 1964 report linking smoking to cancer, was a trusted government agency. Research shows that even truthful information will be dismissed by audiences if it does not come from a trusted source. Responsibility for warning the public about disinformation threats should fall to the Department of Homeland Security (DHS) and the Federal Emergency Management Agency (FEMA), which are responsible for providing accurate information during crises.

Third, even though the US government led the campaign to curtail smoking, it also sought help from the private sector. Today, civil society groups are developing innovative techniques for exposing disinformation, but these efforts are nascent and strapped for resources. The State Department's Global Engagement Center is the only US government entity with a mandate to counter disinformation.

Fourth, the Education Department should work closely with states to reinvigorate civics education for the digital age. "Just as we teach children about the health risks associated with smoking, we should also educate them to become critical consumers of information. Only a whole-of-society approach—one that engages government, private companies and civil society alike—can effectively combat and build resilience to disinformation" (Polyakova & Gonzalez, 2018).

Durkin, Biener, and Wakefield (2009) studied the effects of different types of antismoking ads on reducing disparities in smoking cessation among socioeconomic subgroups:

Smokers were exposed to more than 200 antismoking ads during the 2-year period. The odds of having quit at follow-up increased by 11% with each 10 additional potential ad exposures. Greater exposure to ads that contained highly emotional elements or personal stories drove this effect, which was greater among respondents with low and mid-socioeconomic status than among high–socioeconomic status groups. Emotionally evocative ads and ads that contain personalized stories about the effects of smoking and quitting hold promise for efforts to promote smoking cessation and reduce socioeconomic disparities in smoking. (Durkin, Biener, & Wakefield, 2009)

The implications are that messaging aimed at mitigating misinformation and disinformation will need to be tailored to different populations. The advertising industry has long known the importance of such tailoring. Addressing this challenge will need commensurate deep knowledge of different constituencies. I return to this in Chapter 7.

Gaining and Sustaining Support

The process for gaining and sustaining stakeholder support is shown in Figure 4.5. This process embodies the principles of human-centered design discussed in Chapter 2. Trust is central to addressing the types of challenges of interest in this book. Stakeholders need to understand and support a shared vision. Indeed, they need to contribute to this shared vision.

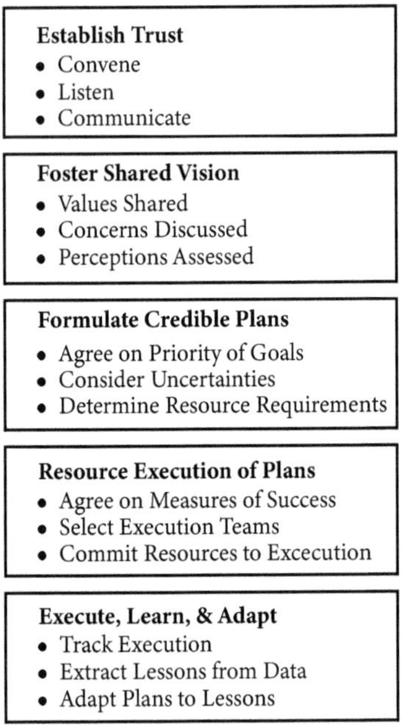

Establish Trust
- Convene
- Listen
- Communicate

Foster Shared Vision
- Values Shared
- Concerns Discussed
- Perceptions Assessed

Formulate Credible Plans
- Agree on Priority of Goals
- Consider Uncertainties
- Determine Resource Requirements

Resource Execution of Plans
- Agree on Measures of Success
- Select Execution Teams
- Commit Resources to Excecution

Execute, Learn, & Adapt
- Track Execution
- Extract Lessons from Data
- Adapt Plans to Lessons

Figure 4.5 Gaining and Sustaining Stakeholder Support

There needs to be credible plans for progressing. People need to believe plans are likely to succeed. Central to such beliefs are perceptions that resources are adequate and committed to success. Perceptions that plans are under-resourced, in terms of human or financial resources, can lead to cynicism and lack of sustained support. Finally, honesty about the needs to learn and adapt are crucial as most people understand you cannot get everything right up front.

My experiences have been that computational models and interactive visualizations can be central to achieving the objectives embodied in Figure 4.5. There are several key elements to this being helpful:

- Stakeholders need to be able to take the controls and run the models with their preferred assumptions
- Stakeholders need to be empowered to ask questions about assumptions and vary them to better align with their perceptions
- Stakeholders need to feel an increased sense of ownership in the computational models as these models reflect their perceptions and preferences

I discuss, in depth, the creation and use of such interactive models in Chapter 5, drawing upon my recent books (Rouse, 2015, 2019, 2021, 2022).

The steps in Figure 4.5, whether computationally supported or not, tend to require significant investments of attention and interpersonal attention. It is not just a process of reaching agreement. Much more discussion, debate, and negotiation are involved. To gain stakeholders' support, they need to be engaged and feel heard and valued.

Change Decisions

A central hurdle to gaining and sustaining stakeholder support concerns getting people to entertain decisions to change and then making these decisions. More specifically, we need to get private and public sector decision-makers to embrace the change portfolio embodied in Table 4.1.

We need to address the behavioral and social nature of decision-making. People often react to incentives and rewards rather than values and principles. They do not like to admit they are wrong (e.g., misread market), and do not like conflicts with key stakeholders. People tend to delay major decisions until everyone is on board.

People have various defense mechanisms and limitations. They may deny the situation because it threatens the status quo, including various rice bowls. They may deny acknowledging the situation because it would not be socially unacceptable for their reputation or the mood of the organization.

They may distance themselves from the situation due to temporal and spatial discounting. The consequences may be delayed and they can discount them, perhaps because they are unlikely to be there when the consequences are manifested (Story et al., 2014). They may spatially discount the consequences because they will be manifested far away.

Managers may have attention deficits due to preoccupation with the status quo, or what Hallowell (2005) terms an attention deficit trait such that "an event occurs when a manager is desperately trying to deal with more input than he possibly can. In survival mode, the manager makes impulsive judgments, angrily rushing to bring closure to whatever matter is at hand. He feels compelled to get the problem under control immediately, to extinguish the perceived danger lest it destroy him."

Figure 4.6 summarizes these observations on decision-making by executives who decide where to invest resources and managers who oversee operations. The economic and social environments have enormous impacts, beyond the symptoms and contingencies of the failures anticipated or at hand. There are significant consequences for where and how the organization invests and manages.

Is it important that organizations accurately assess the strategic situation they are facing, including any current failure situation? Our studies of the former suggest that strategic situation assessment is

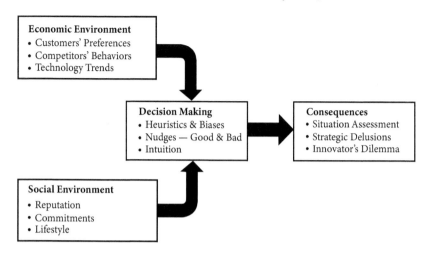

Figure 4.6 Factors Affecting Decision-Making and Consequences

often badly flawed (Rouse, 1996). It is quite common for executives and managers to assume, often only implicitly, that they are in the same situation that led to their past successes.

Our studies of delusions that undermine strategic thinking (Rouse, 1998) suggest other possible difficulties in addressing failures. One delusion is "we just have to make our numbers." Production and performance are paramount. All the processes are in place to achieve this safely. This reflects the delusion that "we have the ducks all aligned." The key is that organizations make implicit assumptions that are no longer justified, but are seldom questioned (Harford, 2011).

Christensen (1997) has addressed a major consequence of inaccurate situation assessments and strategic delusions in terms of the innovator's dilemma. He has studied this phenomenon in business, healthcare, and education. Succinctly, inventions that could become significant market innovations are ignored because they cannot yet compete with the status quo in terms of near-term revenues and profits.

These limitations can be systematically overcome—once one realizes why these hurdles emerge and how they can be mitigated. These hurdles "come with the territory." I return to this in later chapters.

Conclusions

With this chapter, we are halfway through **Beyond Quick Fixes**. Let's review our course of travel. In Chapter 1, we discussed how citizens and leaders are frustrated by one seemingly overwhelming challenge after another. They occasionally muster the gumption for a quick fix, but success is rare. These challenges are epitomized by health, education, energy, and mis/disinformation, with the latter exacerbating all the challenges.

In Chapter 2, we addressed the need to approach these challenges in a different way. Building on understanding from economic, behavioral, and social sciences, as well as political science and history, we formulated wicked problems as complex adaptive systems addressable by human-centered design. This integrated approach moves far beyond transitional engineering.

Chapter 3 considered the need to understand the stakeholders associated with the challenges in terms of their values, concerns, and perceptions. Our intent is to enhance human abilities, overcome human limitations, and foster human acceptance. This requires an extraordinarily proactive engagement of stakeholders. We summarized the stakeholders in each challenge domain, as well as the multi-level structure of each domain. We considered interaction among the challenges.

Chapter 4—this chapter—formulated long-term, multi-stage plans for addressing challenges and their interactions. By long-term, I mean decades, not years. Yet, the multi-stage plans will enable some early, albeit modest, wins that will provide stakeholders confidence that progress is being made. Sustained stakeholder engagement is central to overall success.

To overcome perceptions that these visions and plans are unrealistically optimistic, I reviewed past successes by positive deviants who moved beyond norms to accomplish admirable successes. The central message is: We know how to do this and have done it before! Success will require aggressive marketing and sales plans, as well as assured significant and sustained resources.

So, where are we headed? Chapter 5 is primarily concerned with how all the pieces fit together. There are not four disparate challenges—they all fit and play together. Beyond common objectives and functional needs, they can be enhanced by decision support and intelligent systems technology. Human-centered support is both imaginable and feasible.

I address this integration as a human-centered design problem. Stakeholders' attributes and preferences are addressed at multiple levels. At the highest level, stakeholders are concerned with health and education outcomes, energy availability, and trusted information sources. At a lower level, stakeholders are more focused on the information infrastructure that enables these outcomes.

The design of this infrastructure can be greatly enhanced by the appropriate use of decision support and intelligent systems technology. I elaborate on the functional needs this technology can provide. Two use case scenarios are provided, one involving driverless cars for people with disabilities, and the other focused on cognitive assistance for clinicians. I discuss the ways in which these two scenarios address the four challenges.

Chapter 6 focuses on the economic realities of pursuing the functionality elaborated in Chapter 5. There will be revenue generated and costs saved over decades. The accounting for these cash flows needs to cross agencies and, of course, years. We are not only concerned with next year's budget, but next decade's society. Economic integration is a key to affordable change. The economic model that I present considers the investments and returns associated with addressing the challenges in an integrated manner.

Chapter 7 addresses the need to continually motivate and resource ongoing change, which requires understanding and balancing economics across silos and ecosystems. We need to circumvent the "valley of death" whereby successful pilot tests are not scaled and sustained. Beyond proving the benefits for small, targeted populations, sustained motivation and resources are needed to benefit everybody. I discuss the genesis of social movements and such possibilities relative to the challenges addressed in this book.

In Chapter 8, the whole line of reasoning is brought together by focusing on organizational and personal change. Learning and growth are central, requiring reflection and immersion. This has to be pursued while successfully responding to a set of ten natural and human-made challenges. The emphasis is on translating compelling and coherent visions and plans into demonstrable and attractive societal successes.

References

Barnes, R., & Marimow, A.E. (2022). A landmark Supreme Court fight over social media now looks likely. *Washington Post*, September 19.

Chou, W.S., Oh, A., & Klein, W.M.P. (2018). Addressing health-related misinformation on social media. *Journal of the American Medical Association*, 320 (23), 2417–2418.

Christensen, C.M. (1997). *The Innovator's Dilemma: When New Technologies Cause Great Firms to Fail.* Boston, MA: Harvard Business Review Press.

DOE (2022). *United States Energy and Employment Report (USEER).* Washington, DC: Department of Energy.

Durkin, S.J., Biener, L., & Wakefield, M.A. (2009). Effects of different types of antismoking ads on reducing disparities in smoking cessation among socioeconomic subgroups. *American Journal of Public Health*, 99 (12), 2217–2223.

Economist (2023). Excess deaths are soaring as health-care systems wobble: What lessons can be learned from a miserable winter across the rich world? *The Economist*, January 19.

Gillis, J., & Norris, T.H. (2022). Here is what is really strangling the energy transition. *New York Times*, December 16.

Hallowell, E. (2005). Overloaded circuits: Why smart people underperfom. *Harvard Business Review*, January.

Harford, T. (2011). *Adapt: Why Success Always Starts with Failure.* New York: Farrar, Straus and Giroux.

Herington, M. (2018). *Energy Access Transitions in South Asia: A Study of Positive Deviance and The Enabling Mechanisms for Social Change at the*

Community Level. Brisbane, Australia: University of Queensland, Ph.D. Dissertation.

Liu, C., Rouse, W.B., & Hanawalt, E. (2018). Adoption of powertrain technologies in automobiles: A system dynamics model of technology diffusion in the American market. *IEEE Transactions on Vehicular Technology,* 67 (7), 5621–5634.

Mathews, J. (2017). Downtrodden parts of Texas lead nation in challenging high school students. *Washington Post,* May 26.

Mathews, J. (2021). *An Optimist's Guide to American Public Education.* Arcadia, CA: Santa Anita Publishing.

McKinsey (2009). What health systems can learn from Kaiser Permanente—An interview with Hal Wolf. *McKinsey Quarterly,* July 1.

Murthy, V.H. (2021). *Confronting Health Misinformation: The U.S. Surgeon General's Advisory on Building a Healthy Information Environment.* Washington, DC: Office of the Surgeon General, U.S. Department of Health and Human Services.

Norman, A. (2021). *Mental Immunity: Infectious Ideas, Mind-Parasites, and the Search for a Better Way to Think.* New York: Harper.

NREL (2010). *Solar Power and the Electric Grid.* Golden, CO: National Renewable Energy Laboratory.

Pines, J., Selevan, J., McStay, F., George, M., & McClellan, M. (2015). *Kaiser Permanente—California: A Model for Integrated Care for the Ill and Injured.* Washington, DC: Brookings Institution, Center for Health Policy.

Poland, G.A., & Jacobson, R.M. (2011). The age-old struggle against anti-vaccinationists. *New England Journal of Medicine,* 364, 97–99.

Polyakova, A., & Gonzalez, G. (2018). *Why the US Anti-Smoking Campaign Is a Great Model for Fighting Disinformation.* Washington, DC: Brookings Institution.

Reed, S. (2022). Giant wind farms arise off Scotland, easing the pain of oil's decline. *New York Times,* November 27.

Rouse, W.B. (1996). *Start Where You Are: Matching Your Strategy to Your Marketplace.* San Francisco, CA: Jossey-Bass.

Rouse, W.B. (1998). *Don't Jump to Solutions: Thirteen Delusions that Undermine Strategic Thinking.* San Francisco, CA: Jossey-Bass.

Rouse, W.B. (Ed.) (2010). *The Economics of Human Systems Integration: Valuation of Investments in People's Training and Education, Safety and Health, and Work Productivity.* New York: John Wiley.

Rouse, W.B. (2015). *Modeling and Visualization of Complex Systems and Enterprises: Explorations of Physical, Human, Economic, and Social Phenomena.* New York: Wiley.

Rouse, W.B. (2019). *Computing Possible Futures: Model-Based Explorations of "What if?"* Oxford, UK: Oxford University Press.

Rouse, W.B. (2021). *Failure Management: Malfunctions of Technologies, Organizations, and Society.* Oxford, UK: Oxford University Press.

Rouse, W.B. (2022). *Transforming Public–Private Ecosystems: Understanding and Enabling Innovation in Complex Systems.* Oxford, UK: Oxford University Press.

Rouse, W.B., & Cortese, D.A. (Eds.) (2010). *Engineering the System of Healthcare Delivery.* Amsterdam: IOS Press.

Rouse, W.B., Johns, M.M.E., & Curran, J.W. (2024). Well-being in a digital age. In C. Stephanidis & G. Salvendy, Eds., *Human Computer Interaction: HCI Application Domains.* Boca Raton, FL: CRC Press.

Rouse, W.B., Johns, M.M.E, & Stead, W.W. (2022). *Medical Misinformation & Disinformation.* Washington, DC: McCourt School of Public Policy, Georgetown University.

Rouse, W.B., & Serban, N. (2014). *Understanding and Managing the Complexity of Healthcare.* Cambridge, MA: MIT Press.

Scott, J.C. (1998). *Seeing Like a State: How Certain Schemes to Improve the Human Condition Have Failed.* New Haven, CT: Yale University Press.

Story, G.W., Vlaev, I., Seymour, B., Darzi, A., & Dolan, R.J. (2014). Does temporal discounting explain unhealthy behavior? A systematic review and reinforcement learning perspective. *Frontiers in Behavioral Neuroscience*, 8 (76), 1–20.

Trethewey, S.P. (2020). Strategies to combat medical misinformation on social media. *Postgrad Medical Journal*, 96 (1131), 4–6.

UN (2023). *17 Sustainable Development Goals.* New York: United Nations, https://sdgs.un.org/goals, Accessed 01/16/23.

Verma, D., Rouse, W.B., DeLaurentis, D., Main, J., & Lombardi, J. (2022). *Policy Innovations to Enhance the STEM Talent Pipeline* (Report SERC-2022-TR-002). Hoboken, NJ: Systems Engineering Research Center.

Walton, A.A. (2018). Positive deviance and behavior change: A research methods approach for understanding fossil fuel divestment. *Energy Research & Social Science*, 45, 235–249.

Wineburg, S., Breakstone, J., McGrew, S., Smith, M., & Ortgea, T. (2022). Lateral reading on the open Internet. *Journal of Educational Psychology*, http://dx.doi.org/10.2139/ssrn.3936112.

WSJ (2023). Britain's National Health Service meltdown: The single-payer system is failing patients, with deadly consequences. *Wall Street Journal*, January 15.

5

Integrating Plans into Solutions

Integrating Interventions across Challenges

In this chapter, I address the integration of the multi-stage plans for each challenge into an overall portfolio of solutions for all of the challenges. The concern in this chapter is about how to enable an integrated solution, while Chapter 6 is about the economic value of an integrated solution.

Figure 5.1 provides a multi-level representation of the ecosystem associated with all four challenges and the solutions discussed in Chapter 4. It is, succinctly, a complex service system, held together by an information infrastructure, that will become increasingly integrated, secure, and user-friendly.

Table 5.1 illustrates the ways in which the four levels of Figure 5.1 apply to the four challenges. Thus, the four challenges are structurally similar, despite substantial contextual differences. This similarity enables employing a common computational framework for all the challenges. It also offers the possibility of considering linkages among challenges (e.g., how education affects patients' decisions).

Table 5.2 illustrates how solutions provide benefits to all stakeholders, while also transcending the pursuits of the current stages of plans to learn collectively and be better prepared for subsequent stages of plans.

In order to project the benefits in Table 5.2, Figure 5.1 must be populated with computational models, as shown in Figure 5.2. At the lowest level, people including patients, clinicians, students, teachers, and others, make decisions to consume or provide services. The next higher level includes networks and processes to provide choices to consumers and providers. Service providers make microeconomic

Beyond Quick Fixes. William B. Rouse, Oxford University Press. © William B. Rouse (2023).
DOI: 10.1093/oso/9780198892533.003.0005

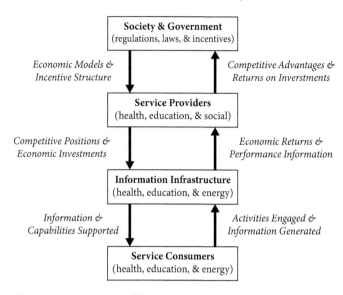

Figure 5.1 Ecosystem of Health, Education, Energy, and Social Media

Table 5.1 Levels vs. Challenges

Levels	Challenges			
	Population Health	Lifelong Education	Energy and Climate	Mis/ Disinformation
Society and government	CMS, FDA, VHA, state regulators	State DOE, local school boards	Federal DOE, EPA, FERC	SCOTUS, FCC, DHS
Service providers	providers, payers, pharma, et al.	schools, publishers, et al.	energy companies	Social media companies
Information and infrastructure	Care capabilities, patient information	Curricula, classrooms	Energy grid, transportation net	Social Networks
Service consumers	Patients and clinicians	Students and teachers	Consumers of energy	Info consumers and producers

DOE = Department of Education.

Table 5.2 Actions and Consequences

Attributes	Challenges				
	Population Health	Lifelong Education	Energy and Climate	Mis/Disinformation
Understanding and benefiting all stakeholders	Patients, families, clinicians, providers, payers	Students, parents, teachers, employers	Consumers, providers, employees	Communicators, consumers, overseers
Transcending current perceptions and experiences	Clarifying and amending hidden assumptions	Clarifying and amending hidden assumptions	Clarifying and amending hidden assumptions	Clarifying and amending hidden assumptions
Fostering ultimate awareness of benefits	Communicating value and pursuit of health	Communicating value and pursuit of education	Communicating value and pursuit of conservation	Communicating value and pursuit of vetted info
Broadly sharing insights with stakeholders	Broadcasting success story to broad audience	Broadcasting success story to broad audience	Broadcasting success story to broad audience	Broadcasting success story to broad audience
Learning that fosters addressing the next challenge	Integrating lessons learned about health	Integrating lessons learned about education	Integrating lessons learned on conservation	Integrating mental immunity lessons learned

choices to invest in service capabilities. Society and government set the "rules of the game" via regulations, laws, incentives, and so on.

These models can be composed into an overall computational model of the ecosystem of interest using methodologies described elsewhere (Rouse, 2015, 2019, 2022). As I later discuss, the abilities of stakeholders to immersively interact with the resulting computational model are central to attracting and engaging stakeholders in the processes of formulating strategies and planning.

Behavioral and Social Phenomena

The models in Figure 5.2 need to include realistic representations of behavioral and social phenomena. To this end, we need to briefly revisit the material reviewed in Chapter 2 on economics, psychology, social psychology, and sociology to gain insights into the hurdles and barriers we are likely to encounter in pursuing the aspirations

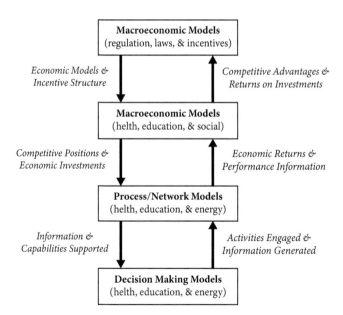

Figure 5.2   Modeling Paradigms Versus Levels

outlined in Table 4.1, including how such phenomena should be reflected in the design and use of the computational environments developed.

Economics has embraced theories that markets know everything and stakeholders maximize expected utility. Hence, their models include assumptions that markets know everything and stakeholders maximize expected utility. Consequently, actual behaviors often conflict with economists' predictions. For example, the value of investments in human education and training, health and safety, and productivity depends on who gains the returns. If returns, albeit impressive, accrue to another organization, the investing organization will see the outlay as a cost and try to minimize it (Rouse, 2021).

Psychological research has shown that humans have limited short-term memory, bounded rationality, and tendencies to satisfice. They exhibit heuristics and biases (i.e., confirmation, optimism, availability, attribution), all of which violate typical economists' assumptions. Intuition, both good and bad, influences decision-making, which is often interrupt driven. Nudges can affect decision-making for better or worse. Training and aiding can compensate for these tendencies.

Social psychology argues that human beings evolved to gossip, preen, manipulate, and ostracize. Social media deputizes everyone to administer justice with no due process. Social media has been weaponized to increase the prevalence and risks of misinformation and disinformation. Polarization and identity politics have strongly emerged, resulting in eroding trust in information and people, as well as institutions. Collective illusions are playing increasingly pervasive roles. Collaborative inquiry is a potential means to address and mitigate these trends.

Sociology addresses societal changes over time, often long times (e.g., humans making a living from their social and natural environment; social and political upheavals associated with the rise of the market economy; origins, nature, and evolution of public opinion). Of particular interest is the long-term transition from the liberal bourgeois public sphere to the modern mass society of the social welfare state. More recently, sociology has come to address key social structures and activities that are organized around electronically processed information networks.

These findings suggest that decision theory models at the people level and microeconomic models at the organization level of Figures 5.1 and 5.2 need to be constrained to reflect the behavioral and social limitations just outlined. Constraints might include limited memory, noisy perceptions, and significant discounting that reflects the realities of human decision-making. The structures of social networks come into play as well. I provide guidance on how to do this elsewhere (Rouse, 2015, 2019). Suffice it to say that ignoring these realities can lead to ultra-rational human behaviors that will undermine the usefulness of any computed predictions.

Human-centered Simulations

The models of Figure 5.1 and Figure 5.2 can provide the basis for an immersive interactive decision-making environment, as shown in Figure 5.3. This *Immersion Lab* includes seven touch-sensitive displays arranged in an 8 by 20-foot 180-degree semicircle. Thus, users can enter into the complexity of their world.

Figure 5.3 *Immersion Lab* and NYC Health Ecosystem

Off-the-shelf software enables one to configure the displays into arrangements ranging from one to seven independent displays. Each display can host one or more models, typically statistical models or computational simulations. In some cases, the models are interactive games. Typically, models on one screen are linked to models on other screens, providing inputs and/or outputs to each other. In this way, users can see how one portion of their world affects the other parts.

The use and value of the *Immersion Lab* are best elaborated with examples. I discuss below illustrative applications in healthcare, education, and energy. The references provided for each application discuss the computational models employed in substantial detail.

New York City Health Ecosystem

The Affordable Care Act (ACA) of 2010 has transformed the healthcare industry. As discussed in Chapter 3, this industry involves complicated relationships among patients, physicians, hospitals, health plans, pharmaceutical companies, healthcare equipment companies, and government. Hospitals are uncertain about how they should best respond to threats and opportunities. This is particularly relevant for hospitals located in competitive metropolitan areas such as New York City, where more than fifty hospitals are competing—many among the nation's best. As discussed earlier, questions that arise in this uncertain environment include:

- What if we wait until the healthcare market stabilizes and only invest in operational efficiency?
- Should we merge with competing hospitals to increase negotiation power?
- Shall we only focus on acquiring physician practices in highly reimbursed diagnostic groups?

In this case study, depicted in Figure 5.3, we developed a data-rich agent-based simulation model to study dynamic interactions among healthcare systems in the context of merger and acquisition (M&A)

decision-making (Yu, Rouse, Serban, & Veral, 2016). By "rich," we meant extensive rule sets and information sources, compared to traditional agent-based models. The computational model included agents' revenues and profitability (i.e., financial statements), operational performance, and resource utilization, as well as a more detailed set of objectives and decision-making rules to address a variety of what-if scenarios.

We applied our modeling approach to M&A dynamics of hospitals in New York City, informed by in-depth data on sixty-six hospital corporations of the Hospital Referral Region in Bronx, Manhattan and Eastern Long Island. The objective of the simulation model was to assist hospital executives in assessing the impact of implementing strategic acquisition decisions at the system level. This was accomplished by simulating strategies and interactions based on real historical hospital balance sheets and operational performance data.

The outcomes of the simulation included the number of hospitals remaining in the market and frequent M&A pairs of hospitals under various settings. By varying strategy inputs and relevant parameters, the simulation was used to generate insights as to how these outcomes would change under different scenarios. The interactive visualizations complemented the simulation model by allowing non-technical users to interactively explore relevant information, to input parameter values for different scenarios, as well as to view and validate the results of the simulation model.

The results from the simulation model facilitated M&A decision-making, particularly in identifying desirable acquisition targets, aggressive and capable acquirers, and frequent acquirer-target pairs. The frequencies of prevalent pairs of acquirer and target appearing under different strategies in our simulation were of particular interest. The frequency level is a relative value in that it depends on number of strategies included and hospitals involved. A high frequency suggests a better fit and also repeated attraction.

Validation of agent-based simulations is challenging, especially for high-level strategic decision simulations. The overall model and set of visualizations were validated in two ways. From a technical perspective, we compared our simulation results with Capital

IQ's hospital mergers and acquisitions transaction dataset. Although there was a limited number of cases under our regional constraint in the Capital IQ's database, the realized M&A transactions appeared in our results.

Second is the feedback from users. There were many, roughly 30, demonstrations to hospital decision-makers and healthcare consultants as well as senior executives from insurance, government, foundations, and so on. In total, perhaps 200 people participated in the demos, and many took the controls and tried various options. They made many suggestions, and the number of types of interactive visualizations iteratively increased.

Two predictions were of particular interest. We correctly predicted the Mt. Sinai acquisition of Beth Israel. We incorrectly predicted that Mt. Sinai would acquire Staten Island University Hospital. Instead, Northwell acquired Staten Island. During a demo to Mt. Sinai, we noted this prediction. A Mt. Sinai executive said that Staten Island was at the top of their list, but Northwell acted more quickly. So, this prediction was not that far off.

The key value of the overall model and set of visualizations was, of course, the insights gained by the human users of this environment. For example, they may determine the conditions under which certain outcomes are likely. They can then monitor developments to see if such conditions are emerging. Thus, they know what *might* happen, even though they cannot be assured what will happen. The greatest insights are gained not only from simulation, but also from interactive visualizations that enabled massive data exploration of hospital performance in highly competitive diagnostic groups.

Economics of Research Universities

This application in higher education was motivated by a desire to understand why education had replaced healthcare delivery as the poster child for runaway costs. Increases in the price of tuition and fees have been far outstripping increasing healthcare costs and, by far, any increases in costs of living. My scrutiny of these phenomena resulted in *Universities as Complex Enterprises* and subsequent articles (Rouse, 2016; Rouse, Lombardi, & Craig, 2018).

I developed a computational economic model for research universities. With its publication in the *Proceedings of the National Academies of Science*, this model was made publicly available and downloaded by many universities. I developed the model to explore how research universities would address three major trends.

The computational model is based on a thorough analysis of a wealth of data pertaining to the various aspects of a university enterprise. This includes sources of funding, alternative publication outlets, predictors of brand value (and hence rankings), workforce structure, administrative practices, and the like.

In this model, student applications are driven by tuition and brand value. While expected degree completion time and potential job opportunities play a role, tuition and brand value dominate. Accepted students who enroll, as well as continuing students, determine needs for classes and faculty members to teach these classes, which drives the costs of teaching. Tenure track (TT) faculty members need to pursue research to achieve tenure and promotion. They need to write proposals to attract funding for their research.

The research activities of TT faculty members result in publishing research articles, which are eventually cited and, over time, increase faculty members' *h-index*, that is, the number of articles cited at least *h* times. The combination of articles published, citations of these articles, and *h-index*, over time, provide an estimate of brand value, which correlates closely with an institution's rankings. This estimate is not a monetary value, but rather a composite performance indicator.

This is all complicated by several phenomena. Research funding is increasingly competitive, with funding decreasing relative to a steadily increasing number of proposals. Publication is increasingly competitive, with opportunities very constrained relative to a steadily increasing number of submissions. The result is that faculty members have to work harder to achieve less success.

Revenue comes from tuition, research grants, and endowment earnings, as well as state budgets for public universities. Costs include those for teaching, research, administration, and overhead. Projections of revenues and costs yield model outputs that include various financial metrics, numbers of students and faculty, and brand value. University leaders have quickly found that cost versus reputation is a very central issue.

The tradeoff is very clear. Reducing the percent TT lowers costs and, in principle at least, decreases tuition. Increasing percent TT increases costs and tuition but enhances brand value. Prospective students seek lower net tuition and higher brand value. Leaders of research universities have to decide where to position themselves relative to this tradeoff.

There are three scenarios of particular interest that may play out independently but have a combined effect on the results projected by the model:

- S1: Status Quo
- S2: Graduate Student Population Declines by 5% Annually
- S3: Graduate Tuition Declines to $10,000 Due to Online Offerings

Note that class size was varied—to 10× or 1000—for the three instances of S3 rather than adding a fourth and fifth scenario.

S3 is the worst scenario, resulting in negative net present value (NPV) of deficits for everyone, because the number of students does not decrease while revenue decreases substantially. Three of the five scenarios lead to substantially reduced numbers of faculty, which undermines institutional publishing productivity and, hence, brand value. The most profitable scenario results when faculty numbers are cut by over 90%. Brand value, of course, plummets and makes all institutions almost equivalent.

Institutions with resources are simply not going to let these futures happen to them. High-resource institutions have been the "first movers" in enabling S3. Thus, they are cannibalizing their professional masters "cash cows" before others do. They are likely to become the infrastructure platforms for others' educational content, although they may also be content providers to resource-poor institutions. This, of course, raises the possibility that these resource-poor institutions will disappear or be absorbed by others.

Overall, all these scenarios result in decreased research productivity due to diminishing returns for S1, and dramatically declining faculty sizes for S2 and S3. All institutions benefit financially by decreasing subsidies for research, although the dramatic decrease in research output should certainly be a national concern.

This economic model of research universities is actually a linked set of seven models. This set of models was hosted in the *Immersion Lab* in Figure 5.3, with each model represented on one screen. Academic executives (i.e., presidents, provosts, and deans), were invited to interact with the model and discuss how best to address the three scenarios. Two reactions were notable.

All of these executives were educated in disciplines such as chemistry, history, or mathematics. They had a limited understanding of universities as complex enterprises. Consequently, they were often surprised by relationships among key variables. Fortunately, we had documented evidence for all of the constituent relationships. A common observation among peers from the same institution was, "Look at this. If we increase X, we decrease Y. I never realized that."

The second reaction was frustration. Their ideas for addressing the three scenarios, especially S2 and S3, were often inadequate for maintaining the financial health of the institution. I asked one president, "You seem upset with the results. Do you doubt the evidence on which they are based?" He responded, "No, I believe you. I just don't like the results."

Energy and Transportation

There is emerging widespread agreement that climate change—sea level rise, increased temperatures, and violent storms—are due to carbon emissions from burning fossil fuels. We are faced with the dual challenges of mitigating carbon emissions, while also mitigating the consequences of changes that have already happened.

Global populations are "hooked on energy." Economic development is enabled by energy consumption. Automobiles, meat consumption, air conditioning, and constant connectivity are among the driving forces. How do we moderate these demands without undermining economic development?

Advanced technologies for reducing emissions and mitigating consequences are key, but how quickly and economically can these be adopted? A key question is: Whose incomes and livelihoods are disrupted and how can they be supported to sustain these disruptions? How can investors be compensated for massive investments, now obsolete?

Substantial environmental and energy challenges are driving the pursuit of alternative powertrain technologies, which nominally include engine, transmission, drive shaft, differential, and the final drive. Emerging alternative fuel vehicles are showing their potential to address these challenges. However, the diffusion of new technologies has many complications. We investigated the impacts of individual and organizational parameters on the adoption of battery electric vehicles (BEVs).

We employed system dynamics modeling to create a representation of the automotive ecosystem (Liu, Rouse, & Hanawalt, 2018). Mathematical relationships among different variables were derived. The impacts of government rebates, manufacturer willingness, and consumer purchasing preferences on economic and environmental issues were addressed using scenario analysis.

Three major stakeholders in the California automobile market were considered (government, manufacturer, and consumer). The types of powertrain systems considered included small/mid-size internal combustion engines (ICE), large size ICE, hybrid, BEV, and fuel cell electric vehicles. Near-term impacts of government rebates, both federal and state, were found to be important to launch the market.

However, the model suggested that long-term impacts will come primarily from product familiarity, consumer preferences, and technology competitiveness. This supports the importance of investments in R&D and advertising. Such investments could be augmented by government support of manufacturers or related research organizations. Rather than depending on short-term rebates to consumers, fundamental improvements in technology and infrastructure (e.g., charging stations, provide more resilient ways to achieve long-term growth of this new technology).

BEVs were found to be significantly more environmentally friendly if the electricity used to charge the vehicles was not produced by coal-fired electric plants. As discussed in Chapter 4, green electricity generation will lead to larger and more stable environmental improvements in the long term. Furthermore, pure green electricity production affects CO_2 emissions beyond just vehicles. Totally switching to green energy production in a short time is highly unlikely, but the model suggests the importance and value of paying more attention to changing production to green energy methods.

The transportation industry is facing a revolution similar to when machines replaced animals over a century ago. Humans may, for the first time, be fully out of the control loop of personal transportation. However, this revolution involves considerable disruption and uncertainty. Nevertheless, autonomous vehicles (AVs) will increasingly impact the automobile market.

We mapped various causal relationships during this significant transition to understand the impacts of different phenomena (Liu, Rouse, & Belanger, 2020). A systems dynamic model was constructed, including two different transportation methods (personally owned vehicle and car services) and three autonomy levels (non, semi, and full).

Consumer choices, product familiarity, and acceptance were modeled to represent purchasing behavior. The US auto insurance industry is likely to be substantially impacted by AVs. Vehicle crash rate and loss ratio were considered to calculate the insurance industry's premium collections. Different scenarios were quantified and discussed with key stakeholders. Several important causal loops were identified that will help achieve faster growth of the technology.

With gradually improving vehicle driving assistance technologies, AVs are expected to debut over the next decade. As a revolutionary way of personal transportation, it is very promising from various perspectives, including enriching personal mobility, reducing energy consumption, and dramatically decreasing vehicle accidents. Yet, not everyone is optimistic.

A primary motivation for this effort was to understand the impacts of AVs on the insurance industry. Every state in the US has regulations that limit auto insurance premiums to the costs of insurance claims. Thus, insurance companies do not make profits on premiums. They make money by investing the premium monies until these funds are needed to pay claims.

The model predicts that insurance industry premiums collected will continue growing until the penetration rate of AVs becomes significant. At that point, the frequency of accidents and hence claims will decrease. Once the AV technology takes off, the industry premiums collected will be dramatically reduced.

Another consideration is the likelihood that people will use car services that own AVs rather than own the vehicles themselves. As these vehicles will be highly utilized, the total number of vehicles on the road will be reduced. Thus, the economic scale of the insurance industry will be further reduced, which will lead to decreased premiums collected. Reduced accidents and fewer cars on the road combine to result in substantial reductions in insurance premiums collected.

In many meetings with insurance industry executives, they characterized AVs as a major threat to their industry. Steadily decreasing accidents portend great social benefits, but stakeholders such as insurance companies, collision repair shops, and personal injury law firms will experience revenue losses. Innovations often result in the investors in the status quo suffering, and the complex adaptive system responds accordingly.

These two models were hosted in the *Immersion Lab* in Figure 5.3. A variety of stakeholders participated in discussions of the future of BEVs and AVs. There were often strong opinions and intuitions whose implications lacked merit once tested with the models. Compared to the interactive sessions on health and education, these sessions often attracted people with significant technical expertise in specific technologies. The facilitators had to be careful not to offend people whose ideas had marginal merit.

Policy Fight Simulators

We demonstrated various portable versions of the applications just discussed. In one demonstration at the National Academies in Washington, DC, a participant asked me, "What do you call these creations?" I responded, "Multi-level enterprise models." Her retort was, "Almost no one will understand that. You are creating policy flight simulators." This terminology was immediately endorsed by participants and has endured (Rouse, 2014).

Policy flight simulators are designed for the purpose of exploring alternative management policies at levels ranging from individual organizations to national strategy. Of particular importance is the nature of how people interact with these simulators. These interactions almost always involve groups of people rather than individuals, often with different stakeholders in conflict about priorities and courses of action. The ways in which these interactions are framed and conducted significantly affect the results achieved.

There are eight human-centered tasks associated with creating and using policy flight simulators. This human-centered process considers and balances all stakeholders' concerns, values, and perceptions (Rouse, 2007, 2015). These tasks inherently reflect a participatory design process (Schuler & Namioka, 1993). The result is a better solution and, just as important, an acceptable solution.

- Agreeing on objectives—the questions—for which the simulator will be constructed
- Formulating the multi-level model—the engine for the simulator—including alternative representations and approaches to parameterization
- Designing a human-computer interface that includes rich visualizations and associated controls for specifying scenarios
- Iteratively developing, testing, and debugging, including identifying faulty thinking in formulating the model

- Interactively exploring the impacts of ranges of parameters and consequences of various scenarios
- Agreeing on rules for eliminating solutions that do not make sense for one or more stakeholders
- Defining the parameter surfaces of interest and "production" runs to map these surfaces
- Agreeing on feasible solutions and the relative merits and benefits of each feasible solution

The discussions associated with performing the above tasks tend to be quite rich. Initial interactions focus on agreeing on objectives, which include output measures of interest, including units of measure. This often unearths differing perspectives among stakeholders.

Attention then moves to discussions of the phenomena affecting the measures of interest, including relationships among phenomena. Component models are needed for these phenomena, and agreeing on suitable vetted, and hopefully off-the-shelf, models occurs at this time. Also of great importance are the uncertainties associated with these phenomena, including both structural and parametric uncertainties.

As computational versions of models are developed and demonstrated, discussions center on the extent to which model responses are aligned with expectations. The overall goal is to computationally redesign the enterprise. However, the initial goal is usually to replicate the existing organization to see if the model predicts the results actually being currently achieved.

Once attention shifts to redesign, discussion inevitably shifts to the question of how to validate the model's predictions. As these predictions inherently concern organizational systems that do not yet exist, validation is limited to discussing the believability of the insights emerging from debates about the nature and causes of model outputs. In some cases, deficiencies of the models will be uncovered, but occasionally unexpected higher-order and unintended consequences make complete sense and become issues of serious discussion.

Model-based policy flight simulators are often used to explore a wide range of ideas. It is quite common for one or more stakeholders to have bright ideas that have substantially negative consequences. People typically tee up many alternative organizational designs, interactively explore their consequences, and develop criteria for the goodness of an idea. A common criterion is that no major stakeholder can lose in a substantial way. For our prevention and wellness simulator, this rule pared the feasible set from hundreds of thousands of configurations to a few hundred.

Quite often, people discover the key variables most affecting the measures of primary interest. They then can use the simulator in a "production mode," without the graphical user interface, to rapidly simulate ranges of variables to produce surface plots. The simulator runs to create such plots without the user interface of Figure 5.3.

Discussions of such surface plots, as well as other results, provide the basis for agreeing on pilot tests of apparently good ideas. Such tests are used to empirically confirm the simulator's predictions, much as flight tests are used to confirm that an aircraft's performance is similar to that predicted when the plane was designed "in silico."

Policy flight simulators serve as boundary-spanning mechanisms, across domains, disciplines, and beyond initial problem formulations, which are all too often more tightly bounded than warranted. Such boundary-spanning results in arguments among stakeholders being externalized. The alternative perspectives are represented by the underlying assumptions and the elements that compose the graphically depicted model projected on the large screen. The debate then focuses on the screen rather than being an argument between two or more people across a table.

The observations in this section are well aligned with my findings concerning what teams seek from computer-based tools for planning and design (Rouse, 1998):

- Teams want a clear and straightforward process to guide their decisions and discussions, with a clear mandate to depart from this process whenever they choose.

- Teams want capture of information compiled, decisions made, and linkages between these inputs and outputs so that they can communicate and justify their decisions, as well as reconstruct decision processes.
- Teams want computer-aided facilitation of group processes via management of the nominal decision-making process using computer-based tools and large screen displays.
- Teams want tools that digest the information that they input, see patterns or trends, and then provide advice or guidance that the group perceives they would not have thought of without the tools.

Policy flight simulators do not yet fully satisfy all these objectives, but they are headed in this direction.

Enabling Citizen Participation

In the early 1970s, I was a postdoc at MIT on Tom Sheridan's Community Dialog Project, funded by the National Science Foundation's program on Research Applied to National Needs, which ran from 1971 to 1977. The idea was to use technology to enable citizen participation in discussions and planning associated with societal issues (Rouse & Sheridan, 1975).

The technology was rudimentary compared to today. Each participant had a small handheld ten-position thumbwheel switch. Each device was connected by wire to a special-purpose minicomputer that displayed the tally on a large electronic tote board (i.e., the number of people voting for 1, 2, 3, and so on). I easily remember hauling around this equipment to meetings in my 1969 VW bug. There was a lot of wire!

We developed three applications for use with the groups studied. TAXPKG addressed income tax policy, SOLVER enabled resource allocation, and GRPRNK helped with ranking alternatives. Four in-depth case studies were conducted:

- Income tax policy recommendations by an interfaith group of clergy
- Investment priorities at a large government research laboratory
- Communication mechanisms among staff members at a large university library
- Grading of term projects by students in a freshman design course

We found that participants appreciated what we trying to do. They also liked the anonymity of their responses. Interestingly, the students in the design course quickly made a side deal to trade votes with students on other teams. I was rather amazed at how quickly they understood the dynamics of the process and adapted in just a few minutes.

The interactions among group members were not at all comparable to what happens in the environment in Figure 5.3. Wireless communication is obviously much more convenient. However, the *Immersion Lab* is also limited by the size of the room and the visibility of the screens. How might we handle thousands of simultaneous participants?

I have long been impressed with John King's articulation of election scenarios and results on CNN. Of course, King is broadcasting to viewers, not interacting with participants. It is easy to imagine, however, people connecting to the CNN website and posing questions. Careful design of this mechanism would be needed to keep it from becoming overwhelming.

A fundamental issue concerns the diversity of participants in terms of interests, expertise, and technology skills. This suggests the need for comparable diversity of modes of interaction. Ideally, the interactions would be tailored to each participant. Individualized decision support would leverage each person's abilities, mitigate their limitations, and foster their acceptance.

There are a variety of political implications for enabling citizen participation. One possibility is emergent social movements, as we have seen having arisen from embracing social media such as Facebook and Twitter. I return to consider social movements in detail in Chapter 7.

Decision Support Capabilities

Summarizing briefly, the vision is for citizen participants to be able to interact with the capabilities portrayed in Figure 5.3 on their own laptops at their desks or easy chairs. Such interactions will have to be facilitated in some manner other than by the young woman shown in Figure 5.3—Dr. Annie Yu. In this section, I outline the intelligent decision support capabilities needed.

As discussed in Chapter 2, human-centered design first addresses the desired User Experience (UX), which differs by level. Next, we consider the user interface (UI) in terms of what people can see and do, as I will elaborate below. Finally, we consider the technology needed to enable UX and UI. I will only provide a high-level description of this, with key references.

Consider UX in terms of stakeholders and their attributes of interest. These attributes and preferences have to be addressed at multiple levels. At the higher levels of Figure 5.1, stakeholders are concerned with health and education outcomes, energy availability, and trusted information sources. At the lower levels of Figure 5.1, stakeholders are more focused on the information infrastructure that enables these outcomes.

The notion of decision support has involved many capabilities over the years. At first, it primarily involved providing analytical capabilities not possible for users to attempt without computational assistance (e.g., optimization). Much more recently, the construct of intelligent decision support has emerged. The idea is that artificial intelligence (AI) can provide expert advice on what alternatives to entertain and which to pursue.

This can make sense in highly structured decision situations (e.g., processing insurance applications or claims). However, this approach faces fundamental challenges when decision situations are much less structured (e.g., which house to buy or spousal candidate to entice). In such situations, we are less open to automated decision support and much more open to augmented intelligence. We seek analyses and suggestions much more than prescriptions.

The foregoing sets the stage for my main argument. In many situations, AI will be used to augment human intelligence, rather than being deployed to automate intelligence and replace humans (Rouse & Spohrer, 2018). What functions are needed to augment intelligence?

Information Management. One function will be information management (Rouse, 2007, 2019). This involves information selection (what to present) and scheduling (when to present it). Information modality selection involves choosing among visual, auditory, and tactile channels. Information formatting concerns choosing the best levels of abstraction (concept) and aggregation (detail) for the tasks at hand. AI can be used to make all these choices in real time as the human is pursuing the tasks of interest.

Intent Inferencing. Another function is intent inferencing (Rouse, 2007, 2019). Information management can be more helpful if it knows both what humans are doing and what they intend to do. Representing humans' task structure in terms of goals, plans, and scripts (Schank & Abelson, 1977) can enable making such inferences. Scripts are sequences of actions to which are connected information and control requirements. When the intelligence infers what you intend to do, it then knows what information you need and what controls you want to execute it.

One of the reasons that humans are often included in systems is because they can deal with ambiguity and figure out what to do. Occasionally, what they decide to do has potentially unfortunate consequences. In such cases, "human errors" are reported. Errors in themselves are not the problem. The consequences are the problem.

Error-Tolerant Interfaces. For this reason, another function is an error-tolerant interface (Rouse & Morris, 1987; Rouse, 2007, 2019). This requires capabilities to identify and classify errors, which are defined as actions that do not make sense (commissions) or the lack of actions (omissions) that seem warranted at the time. Identification and classification lead to remediation. This occurs at three levels: monitoring, feedback, and control. Monitoring involves the collection of more evidence to support the error assessment. Feedback involves making sure the humans realize what they just did. This usually results in humans immediately correcting their errors. Control involves the automation taking over (e.g., applying the brakes), to avoid the imminent consequences.

Adaptive Aiding. The notion of taking control raises the overall issue of whether humans or computers should perform particular tasks. There are many cases where the answer is situation dependent. Thus, this function is termed adaptive aiding (Rouse, 1988, 2007, 2019). The overall concept is to have mechanisms that enable real-time determination of who should be in control. Such mechanisms have been researched extensively, resulting in a framework for design that includes principles of adaptation and principles of interaction. A First Law of Adaptive Aiding has been proposed: *computers can take tasks, but they cannot give them.*

Intelligent Tutoring. Another function is intelligent tutoring to both train humans and keep them sufficiently in the loop to enable successful human task performance when needed. Training usually addresses two questions: 1) How the system works and, 2) How to work the system. Keeping humans in the loop addresses maintaining competence. Unless tasks can be automated to perfection, humans' competencies need to be maintained. Not surprisingly, this often results in training vs. aiding tradeoffs, for which guidance has been developed (Rouse, 2007, 2019).

Example Applications

Many of the earlier research and applications of the notions elaborated in this section focused on the operation and maintenance of complex engineered systems such as aircraft, power plants, and factories. The tasks associated with such systems are usually well understood. One application focused on electronic checklists for aircraft pilots (Rouse & Rouse, 1980; Rouse, Rouse, & Hammer, 1982; Rouse, 2007, 2019). The results were sufficiently compelling to motivate the inclusion of some of the functionality on the Boeing 777 aircraft.

A conceptual architecture for intelligent interfaces has been developed and applied several times to tasks that are sufficiently structured to be able to make the inferences needed to support the functionality outlined here (Rouse, Geddes, & Curry, 1988; Rouse, Geddes, & Hammer, 1990; Rouse, 2007, 2019). The notion of augmented intelligence can build on this foundation, with some important extensions due to advances in contemporary AI (e.g., explanation management).

The health, education, and energy case studies that I discussed earlier in this chapter are amenable to this type of decision support. The alternative choices available to users are well-defined and can be characterized as scripts. Thus, information management, intent inferencing, and so on, are feasible elements of decision support.

Overall Architecture

Figure 5.4 provides an overall architecture for augmenting intelligence. The intelligent interface, summarized above, becomes a component of this broader concept. The overall logic is as follows:

- Humans see displays and controls, and decide and act. Humans need not be concerned with other than these three elements of the architecture. The overall system frames humans' roles and tasks, and provides support accordingly.

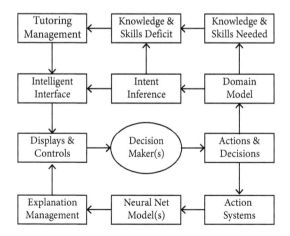

Figure 5.4 Elements of Intelligent Interface

- The intent inference function infers what task(s) humans intend to do. This function retrieves information and control needs for these task(s). The information management function determines displays and controls appropriate for meeting information and control needs.
- The intelligent tutoring function infers humans' knowledge and skill deficits relative to these task(s). If humans cannot perform the task(s) acceptably, the information management function either provides just-in-time training or informs adaptive aiding (see next) of the humans' need for aiding.
- Deep learning neural nets provide recommended actions and decisions. The explanation management function provides explanations of these recommendations to the extent that explanations are requested. This function is elaborated on next.
- The adaptive aiding function, within the intelligent interface, determines the human's role in execution. This can range from manual to automatic control, with execution typically involving somewhere between these extremes. The error monitoring function, within the intelligent interface, detects, classifies, and remediates anomalies.

Note that these functions influence each other. For example, if adaptive aiding determines that humans should perform task(s), intelligent tutoring assesses the availability of necessary knowledge and skills, and determines training interventions needed, and information management provides the tutoring experiences to augment knowledge and skills. On the other hand, if adaptive aiding determines that automation should perform task(s), intelligent tutoring assesses humans' abilities to monitor automation, assuming such monitoring is needed.

Explanation Management

As noted earlier, most neural network models cannot explain their (recommended) decisions. This would seem to be a fundamental

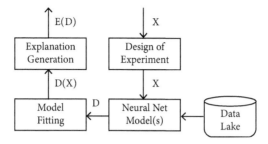

Figure 5.5   Explanation Management Function

limitation (Adler-Milstein et al., 2022). However, science has long addressed the need to understand systems that cannot explain their own behaviors. Experimental methods are used to develop statistical models of input-output relationships. Applying these methods to neural network models can yield mathematical models that enable explaining the (recommended) decisions, as shown in Figure 5.5.

Given a set of independent variables **X**, a statistical experiment can be designed (e.g., a fractional factorial design) that determines the combinations of values of **X** to be input to the neural net model(s). These models, typically multi-layered, have "learned" from exposure to massive data lakes with labeled instances of true positives, and possibly false positives and false negatives. True negatives are the remaining instances.

The neural net models yield decisions, **D**, in response to the designed combinations of **X**. A model **D(X)**, is then fit to these input-output datasets. Explanation generation then yields explanations **E(D)** based on the attributes and weights in the fitted model. The result is a first-order (i.e., non-deep) explanation of the neural net (recommended) decisions.

As noted earlier, the paradigm underlying Figure 5.5 is the standard paradigm of empirical natural science. Thus, it is clear it will work (i.e., yield rule-based explanations), but will it be sufficient to help decision-makers understand and accept what machine learning recommends? We imagine this will depend on the application.

As an example, consider control theory. Optimal stochastic control theory includes both optimal estimation and optimal control.

Determining the optimal solution across both estimation and control involves rather sophisticated mathematics. We could apply the method in Figure 5.5 to the optimal control actions resulting from the solution of this stochastic control problem.

We would not be able to infer the nature of the underlying sophisticated mathematics. Instead, we would likely unearth something akin to classic proportional–integral–derivative (PID) controllers, where the acronym stands for proportional, integral, and derivative attributes of the errors between desired and actual states. It has been shown that this provides a reasonable explanation of optimal control actions.

Learning Loops

Figures 5.4 and 5.5 include both explicit and implicit learning loops. The statistical machine-learning loop will be continually refining the relationships in its layers, either by supervised learning or reinforcement learning. This will involve balancing exploration (of uncharted territory) and exploitation (of current knowledge). This may involve human designers and experimenters not included in Figures 5.4 and 5.5. Of particular interest is how machine learning will forget older data and examples that are no longer relevant (e.g., a health treatment that has more recently been shown to be ineffective).

The rule-based learning loops in Figures 5.4 and 5.5 are concerned with inferring rule-based explanations of the recommendations resulting from machine learning (Figure 5.5) and inferring human decision-makers' intentions and state of knowledge (Figure 5.4). Further, learning by decision-makers is facilitated by the tutoring function in Figure 5.4.

Thus, the AI will be learning about phenomena, cues, decisions, actions, and so on, in the overall task environment. The decision-makers will learn about what the AI is learning, expressed in more readily understandable rule-based forms. The intelligent support system will be learning about the decision-makers' intentions, information needs, and so on, as well as influencing what the decision-makers learn.

Addressing Challenges

How does all of this address the four challenges? First of all, the three case studies in health, education, and energy were all conducted in the same simulation framework and facility. Hence, the capabilities subsequently elaborated are applicable across domains. Thus, we can address all the challenges in similar ways.

I have also illustrated how citizen participation in relevant discussions and debates can be enabled. People can gain the information and knowledge they seek, as well as express opinions and preferences of importance to them. We know how to do this, although we might not yet have the will and resources to do it.

A remaining capability, currently being researched, is how to meaningfully connect policy simulators across domains. Can we validly connect the New York City health ecosystem to the economics of higher education to people's choices of modes of transformation?

At the very least, we need compatible ontologies across domains. An ontology is a set of concepts and categories in a subject area or domain that shows their properties and the relations between them. Relating health to education to energy in this manner is an extremely significant intellectual endeavor that is very much a work in progress.

Conclusions

This chapter has addressed integration plans for addressing the four challenges into overall solutions. The logic underlying this aspiration did not involve the pursuit of a monolithic solution to health, education, and energy. In contrast, the objective is to create compatible solutions. Our integrated simulation framework provides the means to do this.

We next need to address the economic value of doing this. Do projected returns justify the investments required to transform health, education, and energy, as well as mitigate mis/disinformation? The answer depends on how one accounts for investments and returns. I address this in detail in Chapter 6.

References

Adler-Milstein, J., Aggarwal, N., Ahmed, M., Castner, J., Evans, B., Gonzalez, A., James, C.A., Lin, S., Mandl, K., Matheny, M., Sendak, M., Shachar, C., & Williams, A. (2022). Meeting the moment: Addressing barriers and facilitating clinical adoption of artificial intelligence in medical diagnosis. *NAM Perspectives*. Washington, DC: National Academy of Medicine, https://doi.org/10.31478/202209c.

Liu, C., Rouse, W.B., & Belanger, D. (2020). Understanding risks and opportunities of autonomous vehicle technology adoption through systems dynamic scenario modeling—the American insurance industry. *IEEE Systems Journal*, 14 (1), 1365–1374, doi: 10.1109/JSYST.2019. 2913647.

Liu, C., Rouse, W.B., & Hanawalt, E. (2018). Adoption of powertrain technologies in automobiles: A system dynamics model of technology diffusion in the American market. *IEEE Transactions on Vehicular Technology*, 67 (7), 5621–5634.

Rouse, S.H., & Rouse, W.B. (1980). Computer-based manuals for procedural information. *IEEE Transactions on Systems, Man, and Cybernetics*, SMC-10(8), 506–510.

Rouse, S.H., Rouse, W.B., & Hammer, J.M. (1982). Design and evaluation of an onboard computer-based information system for aircraft. *IEEE Transactions on Systems, Man, and Cybernetics*, SMC-12(4), 451–463.

Rouse, W.B. (1988). Adaptive aiding for human/computer control. *Human Factors*, 30(4), 431–443.

Rouse, W.B. (1998). Computer support of collaborative planning. *Journal of the American Society for Information Science*, 49 (9), 832–839.

Rouse, W.B. (2007). *People and Organization: Explorations of Human-Centered Design.* New York: Wiley.

Rouse, W.B. (2014). Human interaction with policy flight simulators. *Journal of Applied Ergonomics,* 45 (1), 72–77.

Rouse, W.B. (2015). *Modeling and Visualization of Complex Systems and Enterprises: Explorations of Physical, Human, Economic, and Social Phenomena.* New York:

Rouse, W.B. (2016). *Universities as Complex Enterprises: How Academia Works, Why It Works These Ways, and Where the University Enterprise Is Headed.* New York: Wiley.

Rouse, W.B. (2019). *Computing Possible Futures: Model-Based Explorations of "What If?"* Oxford, UK: Oxford University Press.

Rouse, W.B. (2021). *Failure Management: Malfunctions of Technologies, Organizations, and Society.* Oxford, UK: Oxford University Press.

Rouse, W.B. (2022). *Transforming Public-Private Ecosystems: Understanding and Enabling Innovation in Complex Systems.* Oxford, UK: Oxford University Press.

Rouse, W.B., Geddes N.D., & Curry, R.E. (1988). An architecture for intelligent interfaces: Outline of an approach to supporting operators of complex systems. *Human-Computer Interaction,* 3(2), 87–122.

Rouse, W.B., Geddes, N.D., & Hammer, J.M. (1990). Computer-aided fighter pilots. *IEEE Spectrum,* 27(3), 38–41.

Rouse, W.B., Lombardi, J.V, & Craig, D.D. (2018). Modeling research universities: Predicting probable futures of public vs. private and large vs. small research universities. *Proceedings of the National Academy of Sciences,* 115 (50), 12582–12589.

Rouse, W.B., & Morris, N.M. (1987). Conceptual design of a human error tolerant interface for complex engineering systems. *Automatica,* 23(2), 231–235.

Rouse, W.B., & Sheridan, T.B. (1975). Computer-aided group decision making: Theory and practice. *Technological Forecasting and Social Change,* 7(2), 113–126.

Rouse, W.B., & Spohrer, J.C. (2018). Automating versus augmenting intelligence. *Journal of Enterprise Transformation,* 8, 1–21.

Schank, R., & Abelson, R. P. (1977). *Scripts, Plans, Goals and Understanding: An Inquiry into Human Knowledge Structures.* Hillsdale, NJ: Erlbaum.

Schuler, D., & Namioka, A. (1993). *Participatory Design: Principles and Practices*. Hillsdale, NJ: Erlbaum.

Yu, Z., Rouse, W.B., Serban, N., & Veral, E. (2016). A data-rich agent-based decision support model for hospital consolidation. *Journal of Enterprise Transformation*, 6 (3/4), 136–161.

6

Economic Modeling of Investment Impacts

Projecting Returns on an Integrated Portfolio

We now need to consider how to integrate approaches across the four challenges, reflecting the reality of their inherent interactions across stakeholders and various constituencies. We need to pay particular attention to creating synergies, as depicted in Figure 6.1. Integration includes leveraging conflicts by broadening agendas to involve new tradeoffs of interest to stakeholders across challenges. We are interested in both the integration of delivery and investment.

Economic integration is a key to affordable change. The economic model in Figure 6.2 addresses the investments and returns associated with addressing the challenges in an integrated manner. Figure 6.2 only includes the money flows among the phenomena in Figure 6.1.

The concern in Figure 6.2 is with money flows over decades. The overarching concern is with money flows across government entities—IRS, SSA, CMS, and others:

- HHS invests money
- DOE (education) invests money
- DOE (energy) invests money
- IRS collects money
- SSA provides money
- CMS reimburses money

Beyond Quick Fixes. William B. Rouse, Oxford University Press. © William B. Rouse (2023).
DOI: 10.1093/oso/9780198892533.003.0006

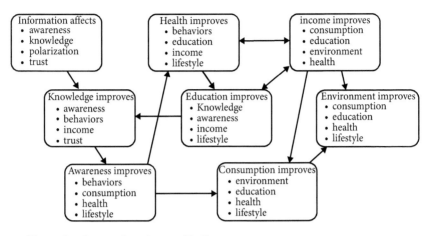

Figure 6.1 Interactions Among Challenges

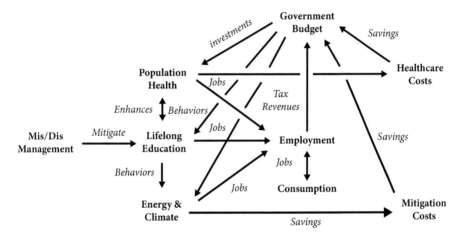

Figure 6.2 Economic Model of Portfolio Impacts

These siloes will undoubtedly push back against changes. However, we want to project the value to the whole country, not to particular agencies.

There will also be disruptions in industries:

- Health—fewer cancer, cardio, and ortho surgeries
- Education—fewer traditional classroom teachers

- Energy—fewer jobs in the fossil energy industry
- Mis/Dis—skepticism regarding freedom of speech

In order for savings to be estimated, we need to project what costs would have been with zero investments. Of course, such a baseline would be politically unacceptable:

- Zero investment in health results in rampant disease and death
- Zero investment in education results in employment being limited to manual labor
- Zero investment in energy results in continued global warming and consequences

Instead, we should consider the baselines we are currently experiencing:

- Continued fragmented fee for services healthcare vs. population health
- Continued fragmented education vs. integrated high-quality lifelong education
- Continued reliance on fossil fuels vs. transitioning to renewable energy sources
- Continued mis/disinfodemic vs. educated and mentally immune population

Overall Economic Model

Figure 6.2 can be simplified to portray the basic logic of the economic analyses in this chapter in Figure 6.3. Investments result in consequences that yield returns on investments that can be further invested. Investment returns accrue to the government, as shown in Figure 6.4.

It will be assumed that any of the cash flows in Figure 6.4 can potentially be invested in addressing the four challenges in this book. Thus, for example, investments in assistive technologies that result in savings to the Social Security and Medicare trust funds can enable

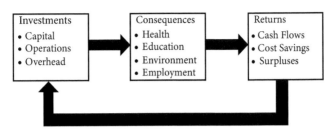

Figure 6.3 Basic Logic of Economic Analyses

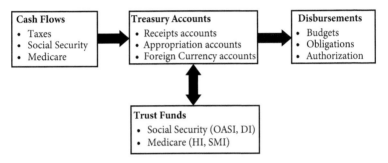

Figure 6.4 US Government Cash Flows

greater investments in these technologies. The status quo rules of the game do not support this assumption, but they should.

In general, savings represent cash flows—lack of expenditures—that can be invested because the savings lead to reduced Social Security and Medicare expenditures. However, the US government does not recognize cost avoidance as an economic gain. The government budgets to cost. Money not needed in the budget simply does not exist. The case studies presented in this chapter illustrate the folly of this position.

Assumptions about employment:

- A percentage of income is taxed
- The remainder is consumed
- Earnings to others, due to consumption, are also taxed
- The multiplier effect is substantial
- People raise children that need health and education investments
- Children become employed and repeat the overall process

I will illustrate this process for the example that follows on the skilled technical workforce.

Economic Modeling

A key to useful economic modeling is a careful assessment of the time series of costs and benefits, especially when considering ambitious and cross-cutting initiatives (Sage & Rouse, 2011). Broader views are better than narrower views, particularly when investing in people (Rouse, 2010). In this section, I define the central phenomena to be modeled and alternative assessment metrics. In the subsequent section, we outline a model applied to assistive technology investments.

There are several cash flows of interest:

- Savings due to investments
- Income due to investments and taxes paid on this income
- Revenues due to sales of solutions
- Revenues due to sales of services
- Profits resulting from sales and taxes paid on these profits

Estimates of these cash flows are used to define three time series:

- Costs over time
- Revenues over time
- Net of revenues minus costs

Money received in the future is not as valuable as money received today, for example, because one has to borrow money to sustain waiting for future monies. For this reason, future cash flows are discounted by the interest or discount rate to calculate a net present value (NPV).

NPV assumes that the projected costs and revenues occur regardless of intervening circumstances. In many situations, however, the results for the first year or two may cause reconsidering the investment, perhaps even exiting the investment. In such situations, one should consider the first year or two of investment as having purchased an "option" in the subsequent years. In this situation, one should calculate a net option value (NOV).

An investment portfolio may include some investments characterized by NPV, some characterized by NOV, and some with both NPV and NOV. Boer (2008) suggests how to value a portfolio that includes some investments characterized by both metrics. He argues for strategic value (SV), which is given by:

$$SV = NPV + NOV.$$

The NPV component represents the value associated with commitments already made, while the NOV component represents contingent opportunities for further investments, should the options be "in the money" at a later time. I later elaborate on the distinctions between the two types of investments.

A very significant issue in these types of analyses is the distinction between who bears the costs of investments and who realizes the returns on these investments. If it is the same entity, interpretation of the results is fairly straightforward. In contrast, if one entity invests and a different entity realizes the returns, the investing entity will tend to see expenditures as costs and try to minimize them (Rouse, 2010).

Finally, health economic analyses often include quality-adjusted life years (QALYs) as an additional metric. In some cases, QALYs are monetized. The technologies discussed in the next section will certainly improve the quality of life for disabled and older adults. However, we lack data for projecting increases in lifespan due to assistive technologies.

Population Health Investments

Having a sense of purpose, maintaining social connections, and staying mobile are often challenges for disabled and older adults who want to work and/or "age in place" but struggle to perform acceptably, both for employment and for activities of daily life. The overall process of investigating the costs and benefits of meeting these needs is summarized in Figure 6.5 (Rouse & McBride, 2022).

This need led to a focus on AI-based assistive technologies (AT) for cognitive disabilities. Two technologies were considered. First, we explored the concept of a human-centered wearable coach that includes both a job coach and a counseling coach. Second, we considered the accessibility of driverless cars by disabled and older adults.

The human-centered needs of these populations were assessed, including implications for AT, by formulating use case models in terms of user experience (UX) and user interface (UI) design. These case studies set the stage for consideration of the economic value of such interventions. Market economics models were employed to estimate potential savings in disability payments and costs of assisted living and nursing home accommodations.

Potential revenues were projected for sales of assistive technology products and services. Contributions to GDP by those benefiting from these offerings are also estimated. In the US, with 100 million disabled and older adults, the annual economic value of these offerings is estimated to be between $150 billion and over $1 trillion, depending on assumptions regarding market penetration. Finally, business case models were used to select among alternative investments by automotive original equipment manufacturers (OEMs). This final aspect of this endeavor in explained in detail in (Rouse & McBride, 2022).

A range of economic issues are associated with the impacts of AT on disabled and older adults. First, consider savings due to more people with disabilities working and increased numbers of older adults aging in place.

Roughly 25% of people with disabilities receive benefits from the Social Security Disability Insurance (SSDI) Program; one in nine also receive benefits from the Social Security Supplemental Security Income (SSI) Program (SSA, 2018, 2019). The average total benefit is $1,335 per month. The total for all beneficiaries is $162 billion annually.

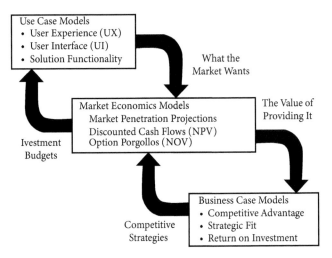

Figure 6.5 Assessment of Technology Investments (Rouse & McBride, 2022)

Among adults over 65 years old, 1.4% live in assisted living facilities at an average monthly cost of $3,600 and 4.2% live in residential nursing homes at an average monthly cost of $8,100 (NCHS, 2019). Total annual costs are $281 billion. Medicaid pays roughly half of this amount. Medicare pays for the first 100 days.

AT can enable people with disabilities to work and, therefore, no longer qualify for SSDI and SSI, creating savings for SSA (Social Security Administration). These forms of AT can also enable older adults to age in place and avoid, or at least delay, assisted living or nursing homes, resulting in savings to CMS (Centers for Medicare and Medicaid Services). Figure 6.6 projects these saving versus percent utilization of these AT capabilities.

The annual total savings range from $44 billion to $222 billion for utilization ranging from 10% to 50%. We do not expect that AT will enable every person with disabilities to work, nor every older adult to avoid assisted living or nursing homes. However, something in the 10–30% range may be achievable.

Next, consider the revenue generated by AT. People with disabilities, as well as their caregivers now working, will generate income,

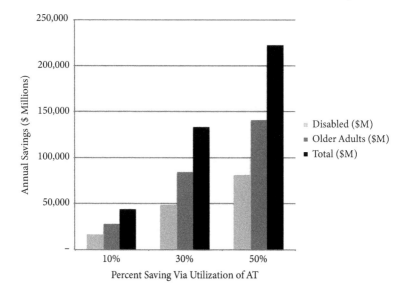

Figure 6.6 Savings Versus Percent Utilization of AT

and pay at least Federal Insurance Contributions Act taxes. In 2016, the median earnings of people with disabilities ages 16 and over in the US was $22,047, about two-thirds of the median earnings of people without disabilities, $32,479 (Kraus et al., 2018). At the lower income, 2018 income taxes were 10% plus 7.65% for FICA and Medicare. For the caregiver earning the higher amount, 2018 income taxes were 12% plus 7.65% for FICA and Medicare.

Thus, the disabled person, now employed, paid the Internal Revenue Service (IRS) $3,891 (17.65% × $22,047) in taxes, while the caregiver returning to employment paid $6,382 (19.65% × $32,479) in taxes. Together they pay $10,273 in taxes. Thus, they were receiving $16,020 (12 × $1,335) in benefits and are now paying $10,273, an annual swing of $26,293 due to employment. This would further enhance the projections in Figure 6.5, although the savings are for SSA, and the gains are for the IRS.

Substantial revenues will come from sales of wearable coaches, vehicle services, vehicle maintenance, and vehicles. Perhaps wearable coach services will be purchased like Amazon Prime at, say,

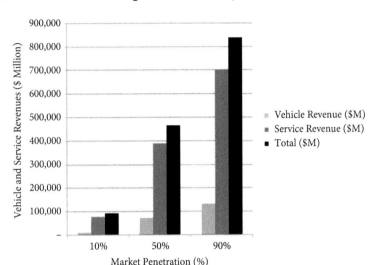

Figure 6.7 Vehicle and Service Revenues Versus Market Penetration

$500 per year, where we assume people purchase their own digital devices. If market penetration grows from 10% in the first year to 50% in the fifth year, revenues will grow from $1 billion to $5 billion. The profit margins could be substantial for this software as a service (SAAS) type of business. However, these numbers pale in comparison to sales of autonomous vehicles and especially transportation or mobility services.

These high-tech vehicles will be expensive, but services dominate revenues because a fare must be paid with each use. Hundreds of millions of trips per week easily add up to billions of annual revenues, as shown in Figure 6.7.

This is clearly an enormous opportunity, with revenue potentially approaching $1 trillion[1] annually if one or more players can successfully address this large underserved market. The successful competitors will earn on the order of $100 billion profits annually, yielding over $20 billion in corporate tax revenues. Further, the $900 billion in costs to a great extent represent salaries and wages that will

---

[1] Recent analyses have confirmed that such projections are quite reasonable (Deichmann et al., 2023; Heineke et al., 2023).

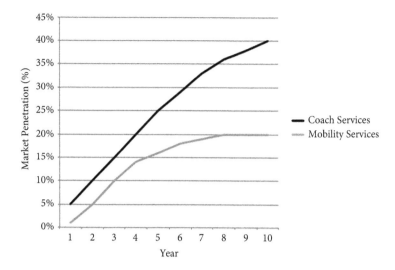

Figure 6.8 Market Penetration for Coaching and Mobility Services

generate perhaps $200 billion in personal tax revenues. Of course, it is important to keep in mind that it will likely take several years to achieve the levels of market penetration needed to yield these results.

The foregoing provides a look at the sensitivity of savings and revenues to adoption of coaching and mobility services. One needs prudent projections, including the rationale for these projections. Figure 6.8 provides projections of market penetration. Coaching services are much easier to adopt than mobility services, and much less expensive.

Revenue projections are shown in Figure 6.9. We assumed a 3% annual inflation and a 5% discount rate. Mobility service revenues are adjusted for inflation. Coaching services are assumed to start at $500 per year and grow at 20% per year as a steady stream of upgrades provides enhanced functionality. It is much more difficult to enhance transportation from point A to point B. Indeed, coaching services may be a primary enhancement to mobility services.

In terms of discounted cash flows, the NPVs for coaching and mobility services are $332 billion and $1,136 billion, respectively. These are impressive numbers, but the key question, at this point,

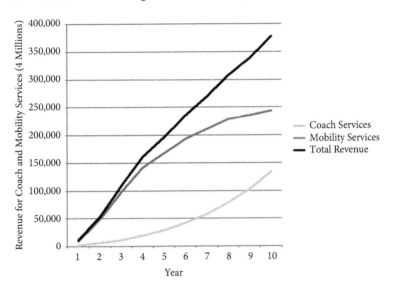

Figure 6.9   Projected Revenues for Coaching and Mobility Services

is what investments would be required to secure these results. This question is pursued elsewhere (Rouse & McBride, 2022).

It is, nevertheless, useful to consider the federal tax revenues that would likely result from these revenues. Assuming current corporate and personal tax rates, the NPV tax revenues would be $66 billion and $227 billion for coaching and mobility services, respectively. These revenues, when combined with the projected savings discussed earlier, make a strong case for societal investment in AT for disabled and older adults. These results strongly support the aspiration for human well-being in a digital age (Rouse, Johns, & Curran, 2024).

Lifelong Education Investments

We have been conducting a series of studies of alternative policies for enhancing the science, technology, engineering, and mathematics (STEM) talent pipeline in the US. This pipeline begins in pre-K, and continues through K-12 to community colleges, to four-year degree-granting programs, perhaps graduate schools, and then employment in STEM or STEM-related careers.

The pipeline leads to graduates who design and develop future complex systems, but also to people who manufacture, operate, maintain and, in general, service these complex systems throughout society. The latter population is termed the skilled technical workforce (STW).

We need the designers and developers of complex systems to be competitive, but we also need the workforce that manufactures, operates, and maintains these systems to succeed in practice, not just in theory and design. We believe that the STW can best be fostered by integrated relationships among K-12, community colleges, and employers.

We have explored how five states—CT, IN, MI, PA, and SC— are addressing the challenge of creating the STW in their states. Our hypothesis has been that fragmentation of such efforts can undermine outcomes, while coordination can enhance outcomes. We identified seven elements of coordination (Gargano, Lombardi, & Rouse, 2021).

In this section, I elaborate on an economic model of workforce investments, as shown in Figure 6.10. Investments in capabilities (e.g., equipment) and operating costs (e.g., teachers), enables education and training that delivers STW personnel to the workforce. These graduates earn income, pay taxes, and consume, creating additional jobs in the economy.

Figure 6.11 shows projected outcomes, assuming the following key assumptions:

- 100 students enrolled and graduate per year
- $5,000 cost per student
- $50,000 income per graduate
- $30,000 income per employee due to a multiplier of 1.7 (non-STW personnel)
- Taxes of 20% of income
- Consumption of 80% of income

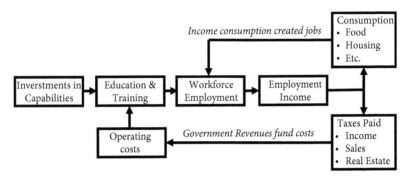

Figure 6.10 Assessment of Education Investments (Gargano et al., 2021)

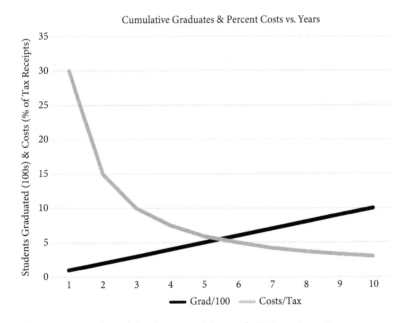

Figure 6.11 Projected Graduates and Costs of STW Investments

Tax incomes quickly dwarf the costs of the STW program. The reason is quite clear. Each graduate pays $10,000 per year in taxes for the next 10 years. Thus, the $5,000 investment in the STW program yields $100,000 in returns **per student**. The $6,000 per year for the jobs created by the multiplier is icing on the cake.

The multiplier effect is well known. The STW graduate earns $50,000 per year and consumes 80% of this income. This consumption provides income to others, who are assumed to not be STW trained and hence have lower incomes, averaging $30,000. These people pay 20% taxes and consume 80% of this income, creating further jobs and tax cash flows. Consequently, tax cash flows continually grow.

This investment decision would seem to be a "no brainer." However, all these tax cash flows include local property taxes, state income, and sales taxes, federal income taxes, and so on. All of these agencies are likely to have other agendas for use of these funds. Consequently, these investors are likely to try to minimize these costs. This will undermine their tax revenues as Figures 6.10 and 6.11 clearly illustrate, but their natural tendency will be to only see this from their perspective (Rouse, 2010).

These two examples from health and education show how an integrated perspective on the economics of potential societal investments enables seeing the tremendous potential returns associated with these investments. The substantial fragmentation of the US systems for health and education dramatically undermines realizing such returns. In Chapter 7, I return to the overarching issue of fragmentation and how we might move beyond it.

Energy and Climate Investments

Figure 6.12 summarizes the energy sources used for electricity in the US. Fossil-based sources account for 60%. Displacing these sources is key to a green electricity future, powering transportation, industry, and homes. The investments needed to accomplish this are quite substantial (EIA, 2022).

Wind and solar will have to expand by a factor of five to displace natural gas and coal. Thus, the number of wind turbines will have to increase from 70,000 to 350,000. At $2–4 million per turbine, this would require $840 billion in investments. Solar power would have to expand to 760,000 acres at $4–500 thousand per acre, requiring $273 billion in investments.

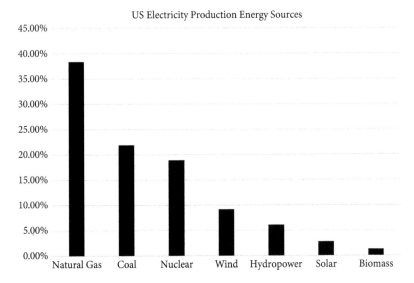

Figure 6.12 Energy Sources for US Electricity Generation (EIA, 2022)

The total required investment is a bit over $1.1 trillion. As a baseline, as shown in Figure 6.13, the total asset value of the top five energy companies in the US is somewhat short of $1 trillion. This comparison is relevant because investor-owned electric utilities serve 72% of US electricity customers. Nevertheless, this investment scenario is imaginable but very ambitious. I shortly consider how savings from preventing and recovering from environmental disasters might contribute.

As discussed in Chapter 4, employment is 7.8 million jobs in the energy sector, growing by 4% annually (DOE, 2022). Around 40% of jobs are in "net-zero emissions" occupations. There are 2.6 million jobs in the motor vehicle and components portion of this sector, increasing by 9.8% annually. The largest percent increases are in electric vehicles (EVs) and hybrids. There are 908,000 jobs in the energy supply portion of this sector, down 3.1% annually; the largest decreases are 6.4% in petroleum and 11.8% in coal.

Currently in the US, 230,000 people are employed in the solar industry and 85,000 people are employed in the wind power industry. Thus, we are at least 35% of the way to creating job opportunities

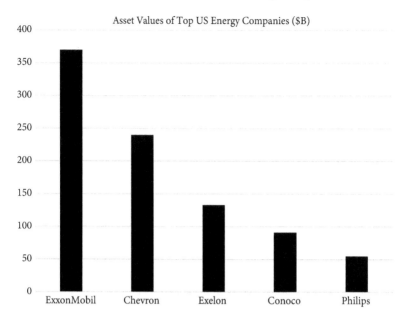

Figure 6.13 Asset Values of Major US Energy Companies

for workers displaced from the petroleum and coal industries. The transition to green employment has started.

A great example noted in Chapter 4 is in Scotland, where wind jobs associated with an ocean-based wind farm of eighty-four turbines provide more than 10% of Britain's electricity, and more than 50% on gusty days. This has created over 31,000 jobs (Reed, 2022). The economic prospects in this arena are enormous (Economist, 2023a).

If we quintuple wind and solar investments as outlined above, it is easy to imagine a much larger green workforce than had existed in the petroleum and coal industries. These workers will earn incomes, pay taxes, and consume, as discussed in the earlier investment case studies.

Nevertheless, roughly $1 trillion is needed. To determine where savings might contribute, consider the costs of disaster prevention and recovery (NOAA, 2023; OECD, 2018) that can be saved if global warming and its consequences are mitigated.

According to NOAA:

> Tropical cyclones, also known as typhoons or hurricanes, are among the most destructive weather phenomena. Since 1980, the U.S. has sustained at least 338 weather and climate disasters where overall damages/costs reached or exceeded $1 billion. The total cost of these 338 events exceeds $2.2 trillion. With the recent addition of Imelda and Dorian, 59 tropical cyclones have caused a combined $1.1 trillion in total damages—with an average of $21.0 billion per event. Tropical cyclones have caused more than half (52.0%) of the total damages attributed to billion-dollar weather and climate disasters since 1980.
>
> Following tropical cyclones, the most costly event types are:

1. Drought, with an average cost of $10.3 billion per event
2. Wildfires, with an average cost of $6.3 billion per event
3. Flooding, with an average cost of $4.7 billion per event
4. Winter storms, with an average cost of $4.2 billion per event
5. Freezes, with an average cost of $3.8 billion per event
6. Severe storms, with an average cost of $2.3 billion per event

OECD (2018) reports almost $1 trillion in damages across 2008–2012. Demrovsky (2022) summarizes, "From 1980 to 2021, the average annual number of weather disasters causing damage in excess of $1 billion was 7.7. A look at just the past five years, reveals a startling increase to 17.8 such events. Our failure to design resilient systems to protect ourselves is costing us money, impeding growth and endangering lives."

There are roughly 20 billion-plus events each year; 52% of events × 20 events per year × $21 billion per event equals $218 billion per year in the US. We should be able, over time, to decrease these costs if we succeed with our green aspirations. If we can save $100 billion per year, we can, over ten years, afford the investments needed to become green, keeping in mind that our trillion-dollar investment will inherently have to be stretched over several years. We simply cannot deploy such resources very quickly.

Thus, we can afford a green economy and a green workforce. However, as with the other case studies, our accounting needs explicit credit for monies saved by our investments, despite the fact that the savings are spread across local, state, and federal organizations. Consequently, we again have to address the phenomena of fragmentation.

Mis/Disinformation Investments

In Chapter 4, I outlined the issues associated with our ongoing infodemic, with particular emphasis on medical misinformation and disinformation (Rouse, Johns, & Stead, 2022). In this section, I consider this challenge from an economic perspective. What are the economic incentives underlying this challenge, what are the societal costs of these practices, and what mitigations are available and likely to be effective?

Economics of Mis/Dis

Consider the broad analysis of the European Parliament (Frau-Meigs, 2018). They focus on the economic incentives for fake news. The top three social media companies (Google, Facebook, and Twitter) had $130 billion in revenue in 2017. By 2021, the total for all players was $153 billion, and is projected to grow to $252 billion by 2026. As an interesting contrast, Apple's revenue was $394 billion in 2021. The US auto industry had sales of $1.5 trillion in 2021. Retail industry revenue was $5 trillion.

Nevertheless, the social media advertising revenue is enormous. Advertising rates are driven by the number of page views of ads. The more people that visit a site, the more page views. People are attracted to Facebook and Twitter because of the outrageous content posted. They tend to "like" or "retweet" outrageous posts. This brings more people to these sites, driving up the advertising revenue. This works to the great benefit of social media companies and the determent of society.

Frau-Meigs (2018) broadly outlines the societal costs, without specifically estimating cost amounts:

- The convergence of mass media and social media creates a combination of interests that can create harm to the integrity of information.
- Risk of harm to the integrity of elections can be due to hybrid threats from part of "information cyberwarfare" campaigns.
- Co-regulation and re-intermediation initiatives pave the way for new ways of dealing with information disorders that can be difficult to adopt.

The health sector is among the most targeted by "fake news," often with real life consequences. An example is "fake news" that emphasized the supposed collusion between the pharmaceutical industry, public health policy-makers and the specialized health magazines, all pushing for unnecessary measures. This is also connected with "science denial," that is most obvious in the plot theories and urban legends associated to climate change. Climate feedback, a scientific initiative that aims at "sorting fact from fiction in climate change media coverage," published a survey showing that half the articles published in 2017 contain elements of fakeness and were more likely to be shared than the others.

Consider a specific assessment of the health implications of mis/dis. Johns Hopkins (Burns et al., 2021) studied the COVID-19 vaccine misinformation and disinformation costs. Their estimate of $50 to $300 million each day translates into $18 billion to $110 billion per year. If the monetized value of mortality and morbidity is included, the estimate is $1 billion per day, of which $60 million is monetary or financial harm. Across the three years of the pandemic, the total cost is over $1 trillion.

John Abramson (2022) reports in his recent book *Sickening* on how big pharma broke American healthcare and how we can repair it. He explains how the pharmaceutical companies have avoided evidence-based reporting and contributed to the US being first in healthcare spending and sixty-eighth in healthcare outcomes. We are spending enormous amounts on things that do not work.

Why is this happening? Advertising of prescription drugs (i.e., the endless ads of happy people), supposedly due to their consuming one prescription or another, only happens in the US and New Zealand. The pharma companies do not disclose their evidence of the efficacy of their offerings to the FDA because of "proprietary interests." The FDA just takes the word of these companies.

What can we do to overcome such practices? First of all, the evidence of the efficacy of a healthcare intervention should not be provided by those trying to sell you the intervention. Second, there need to be standards of evidence, and social media rarely, if ever, meet such standards. Third, the purveyors of misinformation and disinformation need to be liable for the consequences of people believing them. The eventual enormous consequences to Purdue Pharma for the oxycontin epidemic were very slow in coming, but at least happened.

Legislative Mitigations

The US Federal Communications Commission (FCC) regulates the public broadcast media in the US. The Commission has a policy against "news distortion," which dates back more than fifty years to the era when broadcast stations were the only form of electronic news. The FCC's authority to take action on news distortion complaints has always been quite narrow, however. The agency is prohibited by law from engaging in censorship or infringing on the First Amendment rights of the press. Those protected rights include, but are not limited to, a broadcaster's selection and presentation of news or commentary. The FCC's news distortion policy is more narrow than an informal understanding of the term might imply. In weighing the constitutionality of the policy, courts have recognized that the policy "makes a crucial distinction between deliberate distortion and mere inaccuracy or difference of opinion" (FCC, 2022).

Social media, including cable and Internet, are not public broadcast media. They are privately owned, typically by investor-based companies. There are substantial challenges addressing cable and social media that do not "broadcast" (Obar & Wildman, 2015). The social media platforms have the right to publish or not publish whatever content they choose. However, a recent **Washington Post** article reported on efforts to get the Supreme Court to require social media to publish everything (Barnes & Marimow, 2022).

These companies do not want to sell advertisements to customers that may appear next to hateful postings. Would Proctor & Gamble, for example, want advertisements for Pampers to appear on the same screen posting advocating genocide? This ongoing debate is unlikely to be settled quickly. As the EU report argues, a negotiated compromise is likely, with neither extreme prevailing.

Educational Initiatives

There is widespread agreement that mis/disinformation is here to stay. We need to mitigate the consequences of this infodemic. There is also broad agreement that education is the best approach to mitigation.

One approach is to provide people vetted facts. The US National Institutes of Health has undertaken this approach:

> MedlinePlus is a resource created and curated by the National Library of Medicine. Unlike MEDLINE, which is primarily used by researchers and professionals, MedlinePlus is a health information website for patients, their families and friends, and the general public. MedlinePlus aggregates health information from a variety of sources. Some pages, like the medical encyclopedia and drug information, are licensed from outside sources. Other pages, like health topic pages, medical tests, and genetic pages, are created specifically for MedlinePlus. (NLM, 2022)

This makes sense if people ignore other online contexts and rely on this resource. However, online content can be very difficult to ignore without critical thinking skills (Grimes, 2021). The teaching of critical thinking has not been common in US schools, particularly in K-12. However, there are positive trends in this direction.

Norman (2021) has convincingly argued that mental immunity to mis/dis can be achieved by addressing information management via collaborative inquiry, a structure in which members of a learning community come together to systematically examine data, interpretations, and implications. In this way, people can learn to discard mis/disinformation.

Mathews (2015) reports on an amazingly successful program, Advancement Via Individual Determination (AVID), which focuses on inquiry-based tutoring in K-12 employing a well-defined set of principles:

1. Teaching and enforcing orderly learning—keeping well-organized binders, making time for homework, cooperating with other students—can reap enormous benefits.
2. Students can and should be taught how to take notes, one of the most neglected skills in education.
3. Learning standards should eventually take all students, including average ones, to the most challenging courses in high school.
4. In order to push learning beyond memorization and repetition, students should practice inquiry-based learning, so that it will be second nature once they get to college.
5. Regular access to well-trained tutors is essential to bring average students to the point where they can handle the demands of college and the workplace.
6. The demanding college-level courses and tests that have become the measure of high school quality requires that students have support in dealing with them.
7. Applying for college or other training after high school, particularly for average students, cannot be left to overloaded counselors.
8. Programs work best when both teachers and students feel that they are part of a free-thinking family, with students bonding with each other and their teachers.

Since the establishment of AVID in 1980 by Mary Catherine Swanson, it has been adopted by 8,000 K-12 schools in forty-nine states. Around 85,000 teachers are trained annually, and two million students are impacted. Meanwhile, 94% of AVID students complete four-year college entrance requirements, 90% are accepted into four-year college courses, and 84% enroll and stay into their second year. Some 76% of AVID seniors are from low socioeconomic backgrounds, and 86% are underrepresented minorities.

Mathews' books on AVID (2015) as well as the BASIS and IDEAS charter schools (2017, 2021)—see Chapter 4—clearly portray that critical thinking skills can be taught and learned. We know how to foster mental immunity to mis/disinformation. Integrating this objective into these programs would not be at all difficult.

What investments are required to accomplish these education ends? I have seen estimates that AVID costs $1 per student per day, or $150 per school year. These monies are used to pay the highly trained tutors, typically local college students, to serve as tutors as indicated in the fifth principle listed earlier.

We spend roughly $13,500 per student in the US, so AVID would cost a bit over 1% of these expenditures. This amounts to $7.5 billion for 50 million US students. With the costs of mis/dis amounting to trillions of dollars, this would seem to be an easy decision. However, as Mathews (2015) chronicles, school boards, administrators, and unions can be extraordinarily creative in finding reasons for not acting.

Integrated Projections

Table 6.1 summarizes qualitative projections for our four challenges. I provide quantitative projections within the details of each case study. The overall economic returns are very impressive. However, realizing these returns requires that we creatively address the inherent fragmentation of the US economy and society. I take that up in Chapter 7.

Table 6.1 Integrated Projections of Economic Impacts

Measure	Challenge					
	Health	Education	Energy	Mis/Dis	Total
Investment	AT for disabled and older adults	Education and training for STW	100% renewables and green workforce	Monitoring, regulation, education	Healthy, educated and productive population
Savings	Social security and medicare trust funds	Educational institutional efficiencies	Disaster prevention and recovery	Health and consumption behaviors	Repurposing unproductive expenditures
Income	IRS, SSA, and CMS	IRS, SSA, and CMS	IRS, SSA, and CMS	IRS, SSA, and CMS	GDP, growth, effectiveness
Net (10 yr.)	Trillions	Trillions	Trillions	Trillions	Trillions

IRS = US Internal Revenue Service, CMS = US Centers for Medicare and Medicaid Services, SSA = US Social Security Administration

The entries in the cells of Table 6.1 reflect the quantitative examples discussed earlier in this chapter. It would be a daunting task to estimate the economic investments and returns of investing in all health, education, and energy. This would be daunting, but highly valuable. The allocation of societal resources needs to happen in the context of a global understanding of the factors and tradeoffs associated with fostering a healthy, educated, and productive population that is competitive in the global marketplace.

How do these investments reinforce each other? Healthy people consume fewer healthcare services. Educated people tend to adopt healthier lifestyles. Educated people better understand well-being, energy issues, and how to discard mis/disinformation. Correctly informed people will, in general, make better decisions regarding health, education, and energy. For these reasons, at the very least, it makes complete sense to address the four societal challenges with a portfolio of investments.

Uncertainties and Risks

I think the nature and value of the investments that I have advocated in this book make great sense. However, that does not mean they will happen. One reason is that getting Congress to agree on accounting for impacts on tax revenues, Social Security, and Medicare represents an immense hurdle. Accounting for the positive impacts on the Social Security and Medicare trust funds will be controversial as many see cost avoidance as an amorphous benefit. While the US government already borrows from—and repays—the Social Security trust fund, some seriously question this practice.

There are also uncertainties associated with macroeconomic trends. *The Economist* (2022a) recently explored the possibility that strong economic growth will no longer be a priority among OECD countries. They suggest the possibility of retrenchment, noting that "Modern politicians are less likely to extol the benefits of free markets than their predecessors, for instance. They are more likely to express anti-growth sentiments, such as positive mentions of government control over the economy."

Also of concern are forces against globalization, with the US in the lead (Economist, 2023b). Concern about China's growth, particularly in defense-related technologies, as well as US need to preserve competitiveness in markets such as semiconductors, has prompted massive spending by the US government to protect long-held competitive advantages. Increased protectionist policies are likely to be mimicked by other countries.

This is greatly complicated by the emerging consensus that technology innovation is whimpering out.

> After a decade of rising market caps, stocks for formerly hot "tech" companies fell far below their recent highs. This downturn is occurring at the end of record spending on innovation by venture capital firms and incumbents. Futuristic technologies such as quantum computing, nuclear fusion, bioelectronics, and synthetic biology have received massive funding in recent years. Nevertheless, over the past few years, basic economic conditions have become more precarious for many people. (Funk, Vinsel, & McConnell, 2022

Such attitudes will work against my proposals in this book, which amount to a very significant disruption of the status quo. Just days later, however, *The Economist* reported on a new mindset and technology worldview (Economist, 2022b). They suggest that the "cohort of technology eggheads" are seeing things differently. They reflect "A belief that with money and brains they can reboot social progress is the essence of this new mindset, making it resolutely upbeat."

I can empathize with this perspective, although my inherent optimism has faced many tests over the past few years. I think we know what to do, but we need to muster the will to do it. We also need to cultivate broadly based support for these initiatives. Chapter 7 is devoted to articulating a vision for how this can happen.

Conclusions

In Chapter 4, I laid out long-term plans for addressing the challenges in this book—see Table 4.1. Chapter 5 considered how we can integrate these plans into solutions, how these solutions can be communicated to stakeholders, and how to engage stakeholders in the execution of these plans. Chapter 6, as just presented, has been concerned with the economics of these plans. I elaborated on the investments needed and the returns likely from these investments.

I have repeatedly argued that the value of these investments is obvious. We need a broadly based agreement on this perspective. As I just noted, Chapter 7 focuses on this objective. Success in this pursuit will determine the likelihood of our getting beyond quick fixes.

References

Abramson, J. (2022). *Sickening: How Big Pharma Broke American Health Care and How We Can Repair It*. Princeton, NJ: Princeton University Press.

Barnes, R., & Marimow, A.E. (2022). A landmark Supreme Court fight over social media now looks likely. *Washington Post*, September 19.

Boer, F.P. (2008). *The Valuation of Technology: Business and Financial Issues in R&D*. New York: Wiley.

Burns, R., Hosangadi, D., Trotochaud, M., & Sell, T.K. (2021). *COVID-19 Vaccine Misinformation and Disinformation Costs an Estimated $50 to $300 Million Each Day*. Baltimore, MD: Johns Hopkins Center for Health Security.

Deichmann, J., Ebel, E., Heineke, K., Heuss, R., Kellner, M., & Steiner, F. (2023). *Autonomous Driving's Future: Convenient and Connected*. New York: McKinsey Center for Future Mobility.

Demrovsky, C. (2022). The cost of disasters is increasing in 2022. *Forbes*, July 13.

DOE (2022). *United States Energy and Employment Report (USEER)*. Washington, DC: Department of Energy.

Economist (2022a). How the West fell out of love with economic growth. *The Economist*, December 11.

Economist (2022a). How the West fell out of love with economic growth: A serious, slow-burning malaise. *The Economist*, December 11.

Economist (2022b). The new tech worldview. *The Economist*, December 20.

Economist (2023a). Can the North Sea become Europe's new economic powerhouse? *The Economist*, January 1.

Economist (2023b). The destructive new logic that threatens globalization. *The Economist*, January 12.

EIA (2022). *US Electricity Generation by Energy Source*. Washington, DC: Department of Energy, Energy Information Administration.

FCC (2022). *News Distortion*. Washington, DC: Federal Communications Commission.

Frau-Meigs, D. (2018). *Societal Costs of "Fake News" in the Digital Single Market*. Brussels: European Parliament, Policy Department for Economic, Scientific and Quality of Life Policies Directorate-General for Internal Policies, December.

Funk, J., Vinsel, L., & McConnell, P. (2022). Web3, the Metaverse, and the lack of useful innovation. *American Affairs*, November 20.

Gargano, M., Lombardi, J.V., & Rouse, W.B. (2021). *Developing the Skilled Technical Workforce*. Washington, DC: McCourt School of Public Policy, Georgetown University.

Grimes, D.R. (2021). *Good Thinking: Why Flawed Logic Puts Us All at Risk and How Critical Thinking Can Save the World*. New York: Experiment Publishing.

Heineke, K., Kloss, B., von Rüden, A.M., Möller, T., & Wiemuth, C. (2023). *Shared Mobility: Sustainable Cities, Shared Destinies*. New York: McKinsey Center for Future Mobility.

Kraus, L., Lauer, E., Coleman, R., & Houtenville, A. (2018). *2017 Disability Statistics Annual Report*. Durham, NH: Institute on Disability. University of New Hampshire.

Mathews, J. (2015). *Question Everything: The Rise of AVID as America's Largest College Readiness Program*. San Francisco: Jossey-Bass.

Mathews, J. (2017). Downtrodden parts of Texas lead nation in challenging high school students. *Washington Post*, May 26.

Mathews, J. (2021). *An Optimist's Guide to American Public Education*. Arcadia, CA: Santa Anita Publishing.

NCHS (2019). *Long-Term Care Providers and Service Users in the United States, 2015–16*. Atlanta, GA: Centers for Disease Control and Prevention. Office of Vital and Health Statistics.

NLM (2022). *Collection Development Guidelines of the National Library of Medicine*. Bethesda, MD: U.S. National Library of Medicine.

NOAA (2023). *Billion-Dollar Disasters: Calculating the Costs*. Washington, DC: National Oceanic and Atmospheric Administration, National Centers for Environmental Information.

Norman, A. (2021). *Mental Immunity: Infectious Ideas, Mind-Parasites, and the Search for a Better Way to Think*. New York: Harper.

Obar, J.A., & Wildman, S. (2015). Social media definition and the governance challenge. *Telecommunications Policy*, 39 (9), 745–750.

OECD (2018). *Assessing the Real Cost of Disasters: The Need for Better Evidence, OECD Reviews of Risk Management Policies*. Paris: OECD Publishing, https://doi.org/10.1787/9789264298798-en.

Reed, S. (2022). Giant wind farms arise off Scotland, easing the pain of oil's decline. *New York Times*, November 27.

Rouse, W.B., Ed., (2010). *The Economics of Human Systems Integration: Valuation of Investments in People's Training and Education, Safety and Health, and Work Productivity*. New York: John Wiley.

Rouse, W.B., Johns, M.M.E., & Curran, J.W. (2024). Well-being in a digital age. In C. Stephanidis & G. Salvendy, Eds., *Human Computer Interaction: HCI Application Domains*. Boca Raton, FL: CRC Press.

Rouse, W.B., Johns, M.M.E., & Stead, W.W. (2022). *Medical Misinformation & Disinformation*. Washington, DC: McCourt School of Public Policy, Georgetown University.

Rouse, W.B., & McBride, D.K. (2022). Assistive technologies for disabled and older adults: models of use cases, market economics, and business cases. In A. Madni & N. Augustine, Eds., *Handbook of Model-Based Systems Engineering*. Berlin: Springer.

Sage, A.P., & Rouse, W.B. (2011). *Economic System Analysis and Assessment*. New York: John.

SSA (2018). *Annual Statistical Report on the Social Security Disability Insurance Program, 2017*. Washington, DC: Social Security Administration, Office of Retirement and Disability Policy.

SSA (2019). *Annual Statistical Report on the Social Security Supplemental Security Income Program, 2018*. Washington, DC: Social Security Administration, Supplemental Security Income Program.

7
Scaling Solutions for Broad Benefits

Energizing, Broadening, and Sustaining Progress

We need to continually motivate and resource ongoing change. This includes understanding and balancing economics across silos and ecosystems. The overarching goal is to circumvent the "valley of death," whereby successful pilot tests are not scaled and sustained. Beyond proving that a particular intervention will help a small, targeted population, sustained motivation and resources are needed to benefit everybody. Successful execution is central to transforming inventive ideas into societal innovations.

Thus, Chapter 7 is about progress after solutions are initially "sold" in Chapters 5 and 6. This is a major challenge in contemporary society. How can we get the increasingly disparate stakeholders to engage? What can break through the current intense levels of polarization? There are at least two possibilities. First, there is a threat so compelling that we have to come together to address it. Climate change and its possible consequences would seem to fit the bill.

Second, the potential upside of technological innovation in terms of opportunities, jobs, lifestyle, and well-being are so compelling that everyone is totally attracted to this future. Everyone wants to find a niche where they can contribute to, benefit from, and enjoy the prospects of growth and opportunities for everyone. Of course, these opportunities and potential benefits have to be clearly communicated.

Why might these two possibilities work? First, we have to face the realities that many people will not believe the stories. They believe

Beyond Quick Fixes. William B. Rouse, Oxford University Press. © William B. Rouse (2023).
DOI: 10.1093/oso/9780198892533.003.0007

that climate change is not happening. We cannot counter the apparent trends. Change is not economically feasible. We should stick with the status quo, even if everything eventually falls apart. A major educational initiative will be needed to mitigate these perceptions.

Second, people will not believe they will personally benefit from opportunities. They believe that blue states will gain all the upsides. That the red states will be marginalized. And immigrants of color will marginalize white natives and displace them. The levels of education needed to "get in the game" are not achievable by mainstream red-state populations. Addressing these concerns will be central to the major educational initiative.

Beyond education, what can be done about this? We have to mount a classic marketing campaign to recruit the involvement of everyone. We need a grassroots movement to attract the men and women in the street, not just the political players and functionaries. We need discussions in pubs and coffee shops to resonate with these aspirations.

This is not primarily a PBS, CNN, or even a Fox endeavor. It is something organized by neighborhoods, churches, and schools to reconnect people with their communities and each other. We need to discuss and debate what really matters, not from a tribal perspective but from the point of view of a healthy, prosperous community. This chapter outlines how we can make this happen.

Examples of Success and Failure

The New Deal was Franklin Roosevelt's government-led portfolio of programs, public work projects, financial reforms, and regulations enacted to address the Great Depression. Its three themes were relief, recovery, and reform.

Several agencies created by New Deal programs continue to operate under the original names including the Federal Deposit Insurance Corporation (FDIC), the Federal Crop Insurance Corporation (FCIC), the Federal Housing Administration (FHA), and the Tennessee Valley Authority (TVA).

The largest programs still in existence today are the Social Security System and the Securities and Exchange Commission (SEC) (Wikipedia (2023). New Deal. *Wikipedia*, Accessed 02-01-23).

Thus, pervasive and aggressive planning and execution are possible. In contrast, we have been very slow to address environmental challenges. For example, the US earns a D for resilience to the environmental consequences of global warming (Chiu, 2022). Another illustration—more Americans are moving into hurricane zones even as climate risks mount (Phillips, 2022).

However, as the consequences increase in frequency and magnitude, it has been found that, "Living through a natural disaster is associated with higher levels of self-reported belief that climate change is a problem and a greater concern about what this might do to you and your family" (Sambrook et al., 2021; Koerth, 2022). This is also true for Members of Congress, Governors, and others.

Thus, failures and their consequences can provide the impetus for change. Of course, we risk investing too little, too late. This reminds me of Winston Churchill's supposed comment that "Americans will always do the right thing, only after they have tried everything else." We avoid investing in the future until the need is painfully obvious and we have to try to catch up, expensively, and not always well.

Not all change movements are government-led. Ranging from Upton Sinclair's *The Jungle* (1906) to Peter Singer's *Animal Liberation* (1975), the animal rights movement has evolved for well over a century, driven by advocacy rather than laws and regulations. Plant-based food sales have increased significantly in recent years.

The Bauhaus art and design movement was constituency led. It was a German art school that operated from 1919 to 1933 that combined crafts and the fine arts. Walter Gropius (1919) articulated the *Bauhaus Manifesto*, an approach to design that attempted to unify individual artistic vision.

Klein (2011) meanwhile observes that "anger alone can't sustain action, and action alone can't sustain political militancy." Successful movements require:

- Painstaking organizing and constant meetings.
- Experienced organizers teaching and expanding the circle of competent leadership.
- People making the time to do this tedious thing they claim they really want to do.
- A coterie of intellectuals, academics, writers, and professionals who articulate policy.

I return to these points when reviewing the history of social movements later in this chapter.

Methods and Tools

We can leverage several methods and tools that amplify the benefits of human-centered design, many of which were discussed in earlier chapters. In this section, I pull all the pieces together.

Human-Centered Design

Chapter 2 elaborated on this design construct. Succinctly, we want to design solutions that leverage human abilities, overcome human limitations, and foster human acceptance, all in the context of understanding relevant behavioral, social, and economic phenomena. This results in better solutions that are more widely accepted and used.

The value of this approach is not limited to aircraft cockpits and automobile dashboards. A case in point is the study of human-centered design addressing demand and supply for skilled labor in the maritime sector in Indonesia (Munger & Van Dael, 2020). This provides evidence that the approach works in diverse environments.

As Deming (1982) has pervasively argued, the emphasis needs to be on fixing the system rather than blaming humans. People who do not manage their health well are seldom slovenly. People who are poorly educated seldom aspired to be in that state. Our health and education systems in the US do not serve such people well.

Similarly, many people do not understand the impacts of their behaviors on energy consumption and how that contributes to climate change. Many people believe and communicate the mis/dis information with which they are bombarded, including that related to climate change. They need help remediating these confusions.

Service Science

Human-centered design of health, education, energy, and information can be enhanced by recognizing these domains as service systems and leveraging the methods and tools of service science (Maglio et al., 2010, 2019). Service systems dynamically configure and integrate four types of resources—people, organizations, infrastructure, and shared information and knowledge.

These service system resources create value from multiple stakeholder perspectives. The access rights associated with these resources are reconfigured by mutually agreed-upon value propositions. Service systems create and coordinate actions with others through symbolic processes of valuing and symbolic processes of communicating.

These abstractions provide the basis for characterizing the challenges addressed in this book as dysfunctions of service systems. As articulated in Chapter 4, we need integrated health, education, and energy services. This does not imply monolithic integrated service systems provided, for instance, by government agencies. Government can set the rules of the game and provide incentives, but the private sector will be better at creating and deploying innovations.

Trust Platforms

How can we provide integrated services without actually integrating the organizations? The solutions are information sharing and care coordination. Cantwell and Miller (2022) convincingly argue that

Figure 7.1 Elements of Trust Platforms (Cantwell & Miller, 2023).

the key is trust platforms. As shown in Figure 7.1, creating a trust platform involves much more than just technology.

Cantwell and Miller's Center for Medical Interoperability focuses on the healthcare industry, which needs a scalable approach to quickly achieve trust among stakeholders to securely access, exchange, utilize, and protect valuable data. Without common alignment on core principles and specifications, trust is reinvented with each partner's integration. This tends to be a slow, complex, and expensive process.

Their Center has developed the framework in Figure 7.1 for systematically addressing the multiple dimensions of trust. They have demonstrated scale through a platform approach and implementation of a Healthcare Trust Platform with the Centers for Disease Prevention and Control in the US.

This makes complete sense, but is difficult to accomplish in the US. Proprietary applications, such as the electronic health records provided by Cerner and Epic, are inherently not interoperable. I have even encountered situations where two providers who both use Epic are unable to share patient records. The 21st Century Cures Act of 2016 "requires healthcare providers give patients access to all of the health information in their electronic medical records without delay and without charge." This is a work in progress in the US.

Fortunately, we have a positive deviant in Estonia. Heller (2017) reports that

> E-Estonia is the most ambitious project in technological statecraft today, for it includes all members of the government, and alters citizens' daily lives. The normal services that government is involved with—legislation, voting, education, justice, healthcare, banking, taxes, policing, and so on—have been digitally linked across one platform, wiring up the nation.

This represents proof that trust platforms are broadly feasible.

Enabling Technologies

Technology trends will progressively enable information sharing and service coordination. Online resources are increasingly pervasive although, as noted earlier, consumers can encounter great difficulties distinguishing good from bad data and advice. Professional organizations should inherently be better at this.

Sensors and the data they provide can greatly expand capabilities. This can range from tracking one's steps each day to remote monitoring by clinicians of critical variables related to chronic disease. Monitoring of academic progress is increasingly common, as is tracking energy use.

Data analytics and associated visualizations are becoming more mature and usable. However, consumers' abilities to understand and interpret such portrayals depend on some training. This means that a significant portion of the US population will find this formidable as roughly one-third of the population cannot perform simple arithmetic. Our response to the challenge of lifelong education needs to address this.

Augmented intelligence (Rouse & Spohrer, 2018), as outlined in Chapter 5, will increasingly enable patients, clinicians, students, teachers, drivers, maintainers, and people broadly. Consumers, workers, students, and others will have AI-based cognitive assistants to explain concepts, data, and projections and determine if their users understand what they are seeing and hearing, and acting consistently given this understanding.

As Khanna (2022) has articulated, equitable and affordable access to the above capabilities should be assured. We need everyone to be empowered and engaged despite social determinants that create hurdles. Access to enabling technologies and training in their use should be core competencies for everyone. We know how to do this. Now, we need to make it happen.

Seeds of a New Movement

How can we get people to understand societal changes that are desirable and achievable if they will embrace and support such pursuits? More specifically, how can we energize support for the transformation of health, education, and energy ecosystems to achieve desirable, high-priority outcomes?

In *Transforming Public-Private Ecosystems* (Rouse, 2022), I reviewed thirty-six case studies of transformation, twenty historical and sixteen contemporary. The contemporary case studies reflected targeted initiatives to substantially enhance public–private services. It struck me that each initiative was somewhat "blank slate" in the sense that change often began by reviewing and communicating human-centered design principles to key stakeholders and socializing the overall approach.

What if we could foster a social movement such that society's zeitgeist—defining spirit or mood—was human-centered? First, of course, we need a general characterization of social movements. The following quote from Wikipedia provides a good starting point:

A social movement is a loosely organized effort by a large group of people to achieve a particular goal, typically a social or political one. This may be to carry out a social change, or to resist or undo one. It is a type of group action and may involve individuals, organizations, or both. Social movements have been described as organizational structures and strategies that may empower oppressed populations to mount effective challenges and resist the more powerful and advantaged elites. They represent a method of social change from the bottom within nations. Modern movements often use technology and the internet to mobilize people globally. Adapting to communication trends is a common theme among successful movements. (Wikipedia, 2022)

Examples in Health, Education, and Energy

To begin, first consider examples of movements targeted at just health, education, or energy. Subsequently, I outline much broader social movements that set the stage for an ambitious proposal for scaling the solutions presented and discussed in Chapters 4–6.

Health

Hoffman (2003) chronicles healthcare reform and social movements in the United States. "Because of the importance of grassroots social movements," or "change from below," in the history of US reform, the relationship between social movements and demands for universal healthcare is a critical one.

National health reform campaigns in the twentieth century were initiated and run by elites more concerned with defending against attacks from interest groups than with popular mobilization, and grassroots reformers in the labor, civil rights, feminist, and AIDS activist movements have concentrated more on immediate and incremental changes than on transforming the healthcare system itself.

However, grassroots healthcare demands have also contained the seeds of a wider critique of the American healthcare system, leading some movements to adopt calls for universal coverage.

Education

Van Heertum and Torres (2011) consider changes in the U.S. Educational system over the past 30 years. They argue that neoliberalism has dominated the debate, moving away from the progressive reforms of the 60s and 70s, and making economic imperatives the key focus of schooling in America. They start with a brief overview of educational organization and funding in the US, then move on to an historical analysis of the educational policies and rhetoric of the five presidents that have been in office during this period. They next consider the major trends over the past 30 years including the accountability and standards movement, privatization and school choice, professionalism and accreditation, resegregation and persistence of racial achievement gaps and the changing nature of educational research. They conclude by considering the broader implications of these changes, and the threat they pose to the role of education in social justice, democracy and freedom.

Energy

Hess (2018) considers social movements and energy in democracies:

> An important but sometimes overlooked dimension of the study of energy, democracy, and governance is the role of social movements. Industrial transition movements emerge when there is resistance from incumbent organizations, such as large utility companies in the electricity industry, to grassroots efforts to change the industry. A classification of transition goals can be based on two types of sociotechnical transition goals (developing alternative technologies and ending existing technologies) and two types of societal change goals (the democratization of industrial organizations and political processes and the equitable access to jobs and industrial products). The study of processes and outcomes has implications for social movement theory enabling a comprehensive analysis of the relations among the state, industry, civil society, and social movements that provides insights into causal mechanisms in the effects of social movements on industrial transitions and energy democracy.

Historical Movements

Consider notable achievements in broader arenas in the past. Abolitionism, or the Abolitionist Movement (1830–1870), was the movement to end slavery. In Western Europe and the Americas, abolitionism was a historic movement that sought to end the Atlantic slave trade and liberate the enslaved people. William Lloyd Garrison of Massachusetts founded the newspaper *The Liberator*, and in the following year, he set up the New England Anti-Slavery Society. He was joined by Arthur and Lewis Tappan of New York in forming the American Anti-Slavery Society. President Abraham Lincoln issued the Emancipation Proclamation on January 1, 1863. Over three decades had passed.

The Women's Suffrage Movement (1848–1917) was a decades-long fight to win the right to vote for women in the United States. It took activists and reformers nearly 100 years to win that right, and the campaign was not easy. Disagreements over strategy threatened to cripple the movement more than once. The three founders of America's women's suffrage movement were Elizabeth Cady Stanton, Susan B. Anthony, and Lucretia Mott. The 19th Amendment makes it illegal to deny the right to vote to any citizen based on their sex, which effectively granted women the right to vote. It was first introduced to Congress in 1878 and was finally certified 42 years later in 1920. Over seven decades had passed.

The Progressive Movement (1897–1920) was a political movement interested in furthering social and political reform, curbing political corruption caused by political machines, and limiting the political influence of large corporations. The progressive movement had four major goals: (1) to protect social welfare; (2) to promote moral improvement; (3) to create economic reform; and (4) to foster efficiency. Reformers tried to promote social welfare by easing the problems of city life. Progressive national political leaders included Republicans Theodore Roosevelt, Robert M. La Follette, and Charles Evans Hughes; Democrats William Jennings Bryan, Woodrow Wilson, and Al Smith. Aside from banning the practices of price discrimination and anti-competitive mergers, the Clayton Anti-Trust Act also declared strikes, boycotts, and labor unions legal under federal law. The bill passed the House with an overwhelming majority on June 5, 1914. President Woodrow Wilson signed it into law on October 15, 1914. Almost two decades had passed.

The Civil Rights Movement was a political movement and campaign (1875–1968) in the United States to abolish institutional racial segregation, discrimination, and disenfranchisement throughout the United States. The civil rights movement in the 1960s was a struggle for justice and equality for African Americans led by James Farmer, Martin Luther King Jr., John Lewis, Philip Randolph, Roy Wilkins, and Whitney Young. Nine decades had passed. Yet, one can argue that this movement is still a work in progress.

Social movements often take decades to secure the outcomes sought. One can argue that this is:

> . . . a failure to fully integrate agency and structure in explanations of social movements. A focus on great leaders risks neglect of structural opportunities and obstacles to collective action, while an emphasis on structures of opportunity risks slighting human agency. (Morris & Staggenborg, 2002)

In other words, structures must be amenable to change, people must perceive agency to make changes, and leaders are needed to strategize, organize, and execute. As illustrated earlier, people must also be persistent and patient.

Summary

Social movements have enormously impacted our society. Many, probably most, initiatives never gain recognition as "movements." However, as just outlined, some do succeed, with enormous social, political, and economic consequences. While, as just noted, persistence and patience are keys to success, building a coalition of agents of change can, over time, achieve important outcomes.

By "over time," I mean at least a decade, as noted in Chapter 4. In light of the timelines associated with the above movements, perhaps I should more realistically project multiple decades. Moreover, the key assertion articulated throughout this book is that we need to move beyond thinking in terms of quick fixes.

A Human-Centered Systems Movement

I debated characterizing my vision as a human-centered design versus a human-centered systems movement. I finally concluded that human-centered design is a key enabler of the human-centered systems movement. The elements of the human-centered systems movement (HCSM) are summarized in Figure 7.2. My central premise is that everybody wants our societal systems to perform well for everybody. This requires, of course, that we design and operate these functions as systems rather than as a patchwork of activities.

It seems reasonable to assume that we all want service systems that are efficient and effective, for example, for health, education, energy, and information (Bossidy & Charan, 2009). While the lack of efficiency and effectiveness can result in greater profits for providers, for example, in the health system, the HCSM finds this totally unacceptable.

We should desire integration across service systems to foster synergies across public and private providers (Rouse, 2022). This integration can be technological and procedural and does not require actual mergers of organizations. The HCSM will argue and lobby for policy frameworks that encourage this integration.

Figure 7.2 Elements of a Human-Centered Systems Movement.

Equitable and affordable access to services should be assured (Khanna, 2022). This requires the availability of requisite technologies and possibly subsidized access. The HCSM will foster knowledgeable access to and use of resources that will enable well-informed choices among health, education, energy, and information services.

Continuous learning and improvement of efficiency and effectiveness are central (Deming, 1982). Pursuit of the above three aspirations will result in enormous datasets that can inform improvements in efficiency and effectiveness, for instance, in terms of identifying and remediating usability issues and hindrances of critical importance to the HCSM.

We need to leverage lessons learned broadly across health, education, energy, and information services, both in the US and globally, for example, Estonia (Heller, 2017). Inevitably, some ideas will work well, and others will not. Some will only work under particular circumstances. The HCSM will work to assure that the overall learning system explores and exploits innovations broadly.

Principles and Guidelines

Beyond the elements in Figure 7.2, are there principles or guidelines that can help with these pursuits? Such guidance should eventually be created in collaboration with key stakeholders. However, it is useful to discuss the flavor such guidance might take.

Elinor Ostrom (2015) has proposed guidelines for governing the commons—elements of society that are collectively owned and used by many. The governance of natural resources is her primary concern, including meadows and forests, irrigation communities and other water rights, and fisheries.

Williams (2018) elaborates her rules:

1. Commons need to have clearly defined boundaries. In particular, who is entitled to access to what? Unless there's a specified community of benefit, it becomes a free for all, and that's not how commons work.

2. Rules should fit local circumstances. There is no one-size-fits-all approach to common resource management. Rules should be dictated by local people and local ecological needs.
3. Participatory decision-making is vital. There are all kinds of ways to make it happen, but people will be more likely to follow the rules if they had a hand in writing them. Involve as many people as possible in decision-making.
4. Commons must be monitored. Once rules have been set, communities need a way of checking that people are keeping them. Commons don't run on good will, but on accountability.
5. Sanctions for those who abuse the commons should be graduated. Ostrom observed that the commons that worked best didn't just ban people who broke the rules. That tended to create resentment. Instead, they had systems of warnings and fines, as well as informal reputational consequences in the community.
6. Conflict resolution should be easily accessible. When issues come up, resolving them should be informal, cheap, and straightforward. That means that anyone can take their problems for mediation, and nobody is shut out. Problems are solved rather than ignoring them because nobody wants to pay legal fees.
7. Commons need the right to organize. Your commons rules won't count for anything if a higher local authority doesn't recognize them as legitimate.
8. Commons work best when nested within larger networks. Some things can be managed locally, but some might need wider regional cooperation—for example, an irrigation network might depend on a river that others also draw on upstream.

These guidelines make great sense for natural resources. How might they apply to health and education? Various pieces of the health and education ecosystems are owned by public and private constituencies. Yet, the overall ecosystems are owned by everybody. Clearly, the translation of Ostrom's principles to the contexts pursued in this book will require some deep thinking.

There is an overarching phenomenon that makes a fundamental difference, as articulated by Lukianoff and Haidt (2018):

> How identity is mobilized makes an enormous difference—for the group's odds of success, for the welfare of the people who join the movement, and for the country. Identity can be mobilized in ways that emphasize an overarching common humanity while making the case that some fellow human beings are denied dignity and rights because they belong to a particular group, or it can be mobilized in ways that amplify our ancient tribalism and bind people together in shared hatred of a group that serves as the unifying common enemy.

This distinction warrants enormous attention. Our plans need to emphasize an overarching common humanity.

Meacham (2022) provides a compelling example of this orientation in his recent book on Abraham Lincoln. He argues that Lincoln was committed to what Theodore Parker defined as the "American Idea," which was a "composite idea . . . of three simple ones: 1. Each man is endowed with certain unalienable rights. 2. In respect of these rights all men are equal. 3. A government is to protect each man in the entire and actual enjoyment of all the unalienable rights . . . The idea demands . . . a democracy—a government of all, for all, and by all."

Lukianoff and Haidt illustrate how Martin Luther King, Jr. developed and articulated a similar philosophy. Meacham provides a similar portrayal of King's orientation. These two examples of emphases on inclusivity, including their pervasive impacts, provide ample evidence of what movements require to ultimately succeed, not just in near-term skirmishes but in terms of enabling fundamental change.

Agents of Change

Who will enable the changes associated with the HCSM? Many change agents have been working diligently for many decades. Human-centered design has long been taught in college majors in engineering, computer science, and psychology. These offerings need to be expanded to include business, medicine, law, and policy. Elements of this philosophy need to be integrated into K-12 civics classes.

Historically, human-centered design courses have focused on aircraft cockpits, automobile dashboards, appliances, and other devices humans operate (Norman, 2013). The profound and fundamental guidance provided by this and other classics is essential to safe and useful equipment and devices.

Beyond Quick Fixes moves the goalposts. The overarching goal is human-centered systems for health, education, energy, and information services. Succinctly, the goal is a human-centered society. Thus, the HCSM aspires to enhance human abilities, overcome human limitations, and foster human acceptance across all aspects of social interactions and society.

Beyond education, albeit expanded, community engagement needs to provide many agents of change. This includes parent-teacher organizations, sports clubs, church groups, block or neighborhood associations, 4-H clubs, and many others. Churches can play a particularly important role as human-centered design aligns with many theologies.

Advocacy groups such as the American Civil Liberties Union, American Library Association, Planned Parenthood, United Farm Workers, United States Chamber of Commerce, and many others can be important stakeholders in advocating the HCSM. We are seeking the hearts and minds of stakeholders, not so much their material resources.

The HCSM will seek media coverage, broadly defined, as discussed in part in Chapter 5. This includes broadcast, entertainment, and social media. The human-centered story needs to be told and reinforced. Success stories, as well as unfortunate stories of failure, need to be communicated. These stories need to be packaged as personal, human stories, not statistics.

As noted earlier, committed leadership is a key to success. We need teachers, clergy, and political leaders who deeply understand the HCSM and are committed to telling the stories, articulating support, and expanding the base of support. In my experience, few people find the goals of HCSM unappealing; they are more likely to be skeptical of success. Strong, committed, and articulate leadership can transform these perceptions.

We need to keep in mind the broad changes we are seeking have central political components (Ho et al., 2022). They argue that keen attention needs to be paid to political factors that affect broad-based change:

- Interests—political actors often seek to maximize their own interests.
- Ideas—ideas are beliefs about what is or ought to be.
- Institutions—rules of the game that impact which actors have political power; how power is organized, mobilized, and influences the policy process.

They illustrate this guidance with three examples:

- The UK National Health Service was created in the immediate post-war period, when the Labor Party (with the electoral support of trade and labor unions) won the 1945 general election with an overwhelming majority of seats in the House of Commons.
- The Scandinavian welfare states emerged during a period when labor organizations and social democratic parties were at the peak of their political power.
- The US has consistently failed to legislate a comprehensive universal health coverage program, owing to the tremendous power of interest groups that oppose a national healthcare system, the fragmentation and overall political weakness of labor organizations, and the absence of a social democratic or labor political party (Ho et al., 2022).

Of course, I would argue that these three principles are philosophically aligned with good human-centered design.

Broader Forces

The HCSM will necessarily have to be cultivated amidst several broader forces affecting society. Climate change and global warming is a dominant threat, which has long been recognized (NAP, 2013; Economist, 2019). Fires, hurricanes, and flooding have been predominant news stories in recent years. One of my blog posts was titled "There will be no vaccine for sea level rise."

Of course, I have addressed energy production and use in earlier chapters. We are making significant progress in maturing renewable sources. Employment in these domains is growing steadily. Employment in fossil fuel domains is slowly but significantly decreasing. Thus, the transition to green electricity production is clearly underway.

This transition poses risks for the petroleum-exporting countries whose economic development in general depends on petroleum revenues (Yergin, 2020; Friedman, 2022). These are the same countries where protest and possible violence are latent, and will be exacerbated by declining economic resources. Such subsidies are not unique to these countries. For example, the Home Energy Rebate Program for Alaska homeowners provides an annual stipend exceeding $3,000, partially funded as a dividend on energy production taxes.

Yergin characterizes these changes in *The New Map: Energy, Climate Change, and the Clash of Nations* (Yergin, 2020). The HCSM will inevitably negatively affect stakeholders who, perhaps only indirectly, benefit from the dysfunction of the status quo. Thus, economies whose development depends on profits from fossil fuels will possibly experience not only reduced income, but also increased political unrest.

Another force that will affect the success of the HCSM is the increasing prevalence of identity politics (Klein, 2020). The "us versus them" mentality is in complete conflict with a human-centered philosophy. The notion that a rising tide lifts all boats, attributed to John F. Kennedy, captures a key element of human-centered design.

Those who do not want to see others' boats lifted with theirs will be among those most opposed to my proposals.

These broader forces pose significant hurdles. Nevertheless, we have to proceed if we want to scale human-centered solutions to everyone's benefit. As shown in Chapter 6, we can easily afford these pursuits. Chapter 5 outlines the mechanisms we can employ to overcome such hurdles.

Conclusions

This chapter has addressed a major challenge in contemporary society. How can we get increasingly disparate stakeholders to engage in human-centered approaches to health, education, energy, and information? What can break through the current intense levels of polarization? There are at least two possibilities. First, there is a threat so compelling that we have to come together to address it. Climate change and its possible consequences would seem to fit the bill.

Second, we need to portray the potential upside of technological innovation in terms of opportunities, jobs, lifestyle, and well-being that are so compelling that everyone is totally attracted to this future. Everyone wants to find a niche where they can contribute to, benefit from, and enjoy the prospects of growth and opportunities for everyone. Of course, these opportunities and potential benefits have to be clearly communicated. Also, we need to overcome the arguments of naysayers. I address this in Chapter 8.

References

Bossidy, L., & Charan, R. (2009). *Execution: The Discipline of Getting Things Done*. Sydney: Currency.

Cantwell, E., & Miller, E. (2022). *Healthcare Trust Framework Overview*. Nashville, TN: Center for Medical Interoperability. https://medicalinteroperability.org/, Accessed 01/19/22.

Chiu, A. (2022). He's worked to boost US climate resilience. Amid Ian, here's how he thinks we are doing. *Washington Post*, September 30.

Deming, W.E. (1982). *Out of Crisis*. Cambridge, MA: MIT Press.

Economist (2019). Special issue on climate change. *The Economist*, September 21.

Friedman, T.L. (2022). Putin is on to us. *New York Times*, October 25.

Gropius, W. (1919). *Program of the Staatliche Bauhaus in Weimar*. https://bauhausmanifesto.com/

Heller, N. (2017). Estonia, the digital republic. *The New Yorker*, December 11.

Hess, D.J. (2018). Social movements and energy democracy: Types and processes of mobilization. *Frontiers in Energy Research*, 6, (135). Doi: 10.3389/fenrg.2018.00135.

Ho, C.J., Skead, H.K.K., & Wong, J. (2022). The politics of universal health coverage. *Lancet*, 399, 2066–2074.

Hoffman, B. (2003). Health care reform and social movements in the United States. *American Journal of Public Health*, 93 (1), 75–85.

Khanna, R. (2022). *Dignity in a Digital Age: Making Tech Work for All of Us*. New York: Simon & Schuster.

Klein, E. (2011). The four habits of highly successful social movements. *Washington Post*, October 5.

Klein, E. (2020). *Why We're Polarized*. New York: Simon & Schuster.

Koerth, M. 2022). How natural disasters can change a politician. *538*, September 30. https://fivethirtyeight.com/features/how-natural-disasters-can-change-a-politician/

Lukianoff, G., & Haidt, J. (2018). *The Coddling of the American Mind: How Good Intentions and Bad Ideas Are Setting Up a Generation for Failure*. New York: Penguin Books.

Maglio, P.P., Kieliszewski, C.A., & Spohrer, J.C. (Eds.) (2010). *Handbook of Service Science*. New York: Springer.

Maglio, P.P., Kieliszewski, C.A., Spohrer, J.C., Lyons, K., Patricio, L., & Sawatani, Y. (Eds.) (2019). *Handbook of Service Science, Volume II*. New York: Springer.

Meacham, J. (2022). *And There Was Light: Abraham Lincoln and the American Struggle*. New York: Random House.

Morris, A., & Staggenborg, S. (2002). *Leadership of Social Movements.* Evanston, IL: Northwestern University.

Munger, J., & Van Dael, R. (2020). *Putting People at the Heart of Policy Design: Using Human-Centered Design to Serve All.* Manila: Asian Development Bank.

NAP (2013). *Abrupt Impacts of Climate Change: Anticipating Surprises.* Washington, DC: National Academy Press.

Norman, D. (2013). *Design of Everyday Things.* New York: Basic Books.

Ostrom, E. (2015). *Governing the Commons: The Evolution of Institutions for Collective Action.* Cambridge, UK: Cambridge University Press.

Phillips, A. (2022). More Americans are moving into hurricane zones even as climate risks mount. *Washington Post*, October 1.

Rouse, W.B. (2022). *Transforming Public-Private Ecosystems: Understanding and Enabling Innovation in Complex Systems.* Oxford, UK: Oxford University Press.

Rouse, W.B., & Spohrer, J.C. (2018). Automating versus augmenting intelligence. *Journal of Enterprise Transformation*, 8(1–2), 1–21.

Sambrook, K., Konstantinidis, E., Russell, S., & Okan, Y. (2021). The role of personal experience and prior beliefs in shaping climate change perceptions: A narrative review. *Frontiers in Psychology*, 12, 669911.

Sinclair, U. (1906). *The Jungle.* New York: Doubleday.

Singer, P. (1975). *Animal Liberation: A New Ethics for Our Treatment of Animals.* New York: HarperCollins.

Van Heertum, R., & Torres, C.A. (2011). Educational reform in the U.S. in the past 30 years: Great expectations and the fading American dream. In L. Olmos, R. Van Heertum, & C.A. Torres, Eds., *Educating The Global Citizen*, pp. 3–27. Sharjah, UAE. Bentham Science.

Wikipedia (2022). Social Movement. *Wikipedia*, Accessed 12/8/22.

Williams, J. (2018). *Elinor Ostrom's 8 Rules for Managing the Commons.* https://earthbound.report/2018/01/15/elinor-ostroms-8-rules-for-managing-the-commons/, Accessed 01-12-23.

Yergin, D. (2020). *The New Map: Energy, Climate, and the Clash of Nations.* New York: Penguin Press.

8

Organizational and Individual Change

Overcoming Common and Persistent Hurdles

At this point, we have long-range, multi-stage plans for addressing the four challenges in this book (Chapter 4). We understand what data, visualizations, and decision support can enable pursuing these plans (Chapter 5). We have the compelling economic arguments for investing in these plans (Chapter 6). We have a broad vision for how successful execution of these plans can provide substantial broad benefits to society (Chapter 7). What else can we possibly need?

Now, we need to address the stewards of the status quo, those who are benefiting from how things are and want to thwart our efforts to change things. The overarching issue is organizational and individual change. Learning and growth are central, but require reflection and absorption. This has to be pursued while responding to natural and human-made challenges, including:

- When the competition surprises you
- When we misunderstand the signals
- When no owns the problem
- When the unpopular position is correct
- When secondary issues dominate
- When the organization is in the way
- When personalities trump competence
- When abilities to execute are secondary
- When stakeholders thwart change
- When leadership makes a difference

Beyond Quick Fixes. William B. Rouse, Oxford University Press. © William B. Rouse (2023).
DOI: 10.1093/oso/9780198892533.003.0008

In this chapter, I provide practical guidance on how to sense, understand, and respond to such obstacles, as well as how to interpret them in the context of the four challenges addressed in this book.

When the Competition Surprises You

Consider two surprises for General Motors (GM) and how they reacted, initially poorly but later quite successively. Both illustrations involved Ford surprising GM. The first led to a major failure and the second to a substantial success. Indeed, failures to achieve corporate objectives are quite common in the automobile industry. Not every vehicle is a home run—far from it.

In 1981 GM began planning for a complete refresh of its intermediate size vehicles: the front-wheel drive A-Cars and the older rear-wheel drive G-cars. The GM10 program would yield vehicles badged as Chevrolets, Pontiacs, Oldsmobiles, and Buicks. This program was to be the biggest R&D program in automotive history and, with a $5 billion dollar budget, the most ambitious new car program in GM's then 79-year history.

The introduction of the Ford Taurus in 1985 was a huge market and business success, and a complete surprise to GM. It was one of the first projects in the US to fully utilize the concept of cross-functional teams and concurrent engineering practices. The car and the processes used to develop it were designed and engineered at the same time, ensuring higher quality and more efficient production. The revolutionary design of the Taurus, coupled with its outstanding quality, created a new trend in the US automobile industry, and customers simply loved the car.

The Taurus forced GM to redesign the exterior sheet metal of the GM10 because senior executives thought the vehicles would look too similar. Many additional running changes were incorporated into the design in an attempt to increase customer appeal. The first vehicles reached the market in 1988, ~$2 billion over budget and two years behind schedule.

All of the first GM10 entries were coupes, a GM tradition for the first year of any new platform. However, this market segment had moved overwhelmingly to a four-door sedan style. Two-door mid-size family cars were useless to the largest group of customers in the segment—members of the Baby Boomer generation were now well into their child-rearing years and needed four doors for their children. GM completely missed the target segment of the market. From 1985 to 1995, GM's share of new midsize cars tumbled from 51% to 36%.

The Lincoln Navigator is a full-size luxury SUV marketed and sold by the Lincoln brand of Ford Motor Company since the 1998 model year. Sold primarily in North America, the Navigator is the Lincoln counterpart of the Ford Expedition. While not the longest vehicle ever sold by the brand, it is the heaviest production Lincoln ever built. It is also the Lincoln with the greatest cargo capacity and the first non-limousine Lincoln to offer seating for more than six people.

GM was completely surprised by the Navigator. They had not imagined that customers would want luxurious large SUVs. GM responded with the Cadillac Escalade in 1999, intended to compete with the Navigator and other upscale SUVs. The Escalade went into production only ten months after it was approved. The 1999 Escalade was nearly identical to the 1999 GMC Yukon Denali, except for the Cadillac badge and leather upholstery. It was redesigned for the 2002 model year to make its appearance and features fall more in line with Cadillac's image.

In 2019, 18,656 Navigators were sold, while 35,244 Escalades were sold. Escalade has outsold Navigator every year since 2002. GM had clearly adapted to the surprise of the Navigator. One can reasonably infer that the company learned from the GM10 debacle. Surprises happen. Be prepared.

The Taurus and Navigator were two of the best ten cars we identified in our study for GM, along with the worst ten cars (Hanawalt & Rouse, 2010). Other winners were the 1955 Chevrolet, the 1964 Pontiac GTO, and the 1964 Ford Mustang. Interestingly the proponents of these cars were heralded as heroes but later demonstrated this accolade to be premature as Ed Cole advocated the 1971 Chevrolet

Vega, John DeLorean failed with the 1981 DMC-12, and Lee Iacocca tried to kill the minivan program, which basically kept Chrysler in business. The Vega and DMC-12 made our list of the ten worst cars.

What differentiated success from failure? First, one needed to correctly predict what the market would want when the car rolled out several years later. The 1957 Edsel suffered from an unexpected recession. Second, there needed to be a system development process that resulted in the intended vehicle. This may seem obvious, but capricious decisions by top management were often associated with failures such as the 1982 Cadillac Cimarron and 2001 Pontiac Aztec.

More recently, we studied twelve cars withdrawn from the market in the 1930s, 1960s, and 2000s (Liu, Rouse, & Yu, 2015). We leveraged hundreds of historical accounts of these decisions, as well as production data for these cars and the market more broadly. We found that only one vehicle was withdrawn because of the nature of the car. People were unwilling to pay Packard prices for Studebaker quality, the two companies having merged in 1954.

The failure of the other eleven cars could be attributed to company decisions, market trends, and economic situations. For example, decisions by the Big Three companies to focus on cost reduction resulted in each manufacturer's car brands looking identical, effectively de-badging them. Mercury, Oldsmobile, Plymouth, and Pontiac were the casualties. Honda and Toyota were the beneficiaries.

We worked with Rover on the initial conceptual design of the Mini Cooper, before Rover was bought by BMW, who then brought the Mini Cooper to market. We considered four stakeholders: young women, young men, young couples, and young couples with children. The design differences for each stakeholder were interesting. For example, the back seat plays a different role for couples with children. Young women and men differ in dashboard preferences.

The original design of the Mini Cooper broke the mold and revolutionized the auto industry in this segment. Its clever use of space, compact design, and excellent road handling led to consumers judging it as a fun, affordable, and classic sporty icon. It moved far beyond its roots as a humble people mover.

Much more recently, as elaborated earlier, attention has shifted to hybrid and battery electric vehicles (BEVs). Our studies of BEVs have shown that the industry needs to move beyond federal and state subsidies to grow the market. The increasing commitments of auto OEMs—original equipment manufacturers—suggest that electric drive trains will soon come to dominate the private vehicle market.

Driverless cars—autonomous vehicles (AVs)—are waiting in the wings. The marketplace for driverless cars has been quite complex and turbulent, laced with enormous hype. All of the major automakers are working with a range of technology companies. Investments have been huge, although aspirations have recently mellowed, exemplified by Uber and Lyft selling their driverless car units. Here are the primary relationships (in alphabetical order):

- Apple working with Hyundai and Kia
- Argo AI acquired by Ford and Volkswagen
- Aurora acquired Uber's driverless car unit
- Cruise Automation acquired by GM, Microsoft, and Walmart
- NVIDIA working with Audi, BMW, Honda, Mercedes-Benz, and Tesla
- Toyota acquired Lyft's driverless car unit
- Waymo (Alphabet) working with Fiat Chrysler, Jaguar, Nissan, Renault, Volvo, and Magna

What surprises are ahead? I think the main surprise is that all the hype was just that, nothing more. Increasingly capable sensors and smart software will make your vehicle—that you will still drive—safer and more efficient. Over time, perhaps a decade or so, your vehicle will become capable of driving itself, initially on open highways. Driverless cars will become pervasive at the pace that unmanned elevators become predominant.

What can be done about surprises? No amount of due diligence can eliminate them. Fortunately, most markets are forgiving. I cherish the Corvette but not the Vega, the Mustang but not the Edsel, and the 1959 Eldorado but not the Cimmaron. We like to win frequently, but do not expect championship trophies every year. Even the vaunted Apple had its Lisa and Newton.

Some surprises become market innovations; most do not. However, surprises can also cause others to innovate. Technology failures or shortcomings can prompt investigations of how such limitations can be overcome. The only way for everything to succeed is for all improvements to be only incremental. Personally, I am glad someone thought of indoor plumbing rather than improved outhouses.

These examples relate to energy and the promise of BEVs and AVs. What might be the surprises in health and education? The positive deviants discussed in Chapter 4—Medicare Advantage as provided by Kaiser-Permanente and charter schools such BASIS and IDEA—are likely to be surprisingly pervasively successful. The stewards of the status quo in health and education will balk and defend the status quo. They will fail.

When We Misunderstand the Signals

I have been involved in a variety of engagements with automotive companies over the past three decades. These companies' abilities to understand marketplace desires three to four years in advance is a key element of success. There are several compelling examples of getting this right and numerous instances of getting it wrong.

Beyond uncertainties about customers' future desires, these companies also face considerable uncertainties associated with competitors' likely decisions and plans. I have encountered a variety of instances of automotive competitors announcing major investments that they have no intent to pursue. The companies with whom I was working entertained making comparable investments, later learning they misunderstood the market signals.

Many years ago, I was engaged by the South African Foundation for Research and Development to provide a keynote talk on innovation and then facilitate discussion among the 100-plus workshop participants on their issues and concerns related to launching their ventures. The top concern was the availability of venture funds to get started. We had expected this.

The next morning, we announced a venture fund that would provide $50,000 in seed money based on a one-page proposal. We asked participants if we could help them to complete and submit their proposals that day. There were no volunteers. The discussion shifted to the question of what was holding them back. Everyone felt that forming a company was much too risky.

We pressed them on this. Why were they in the workshop if this was not a top aspiration? They responded that forming a company seemed like what they should do since their first choice was unavailable. What was that, we asked. A secure lifetime position in a government agency or institute. We had misunderstood their signals about venture formation and investment funds. This was actually their second choice.

For many years, I was very active in the Atlanta technology community, attending many events and occasionally giving talks on my latest book. I was able to chat with a variety of highly successful entrepreneurs. I recall asking one high-profile CEO, "How did you come up with such a great (software) idea?" He responded, "We didn't. It took our customers a couple of years to convince us of what they really wanted."

At the time, I was CEO of Enterprise Support Systems (ESS), Inc., a spin-off of Search Technology, Inc., of which I was the founding CEO. ESS developed and sold a suite of software tools and related consulting and training services. Roughly 80% of our sales were to Fortune 100 technology companies, all well-known name brands. Our dominant strategy was to move from division to division of these companies with one division vice president opening a door to another.

Our vision of being a product company like Microsoft with its MS Office Products caused significantly delayed recognition of the demand for and value of our services. We eventually realized that we thought our customers primarily wanted software tools when they really wanted expert users of these tools to help them succeed.

A senior executive at one of our major clients put it succinctly, "I am not at all concerned with the cost of your software or your services. I am concerned with the overall cost of success. Your tools, and especially your services, greatly enhance our chances of success. You may make better profit margins on your software tools, but without your services, your tools are much less valuable."

We validated this message with other clients. It was unanimous. This created an opportunity and a problem. We found that we needed sophisticated tools for customers to feel the pricing of software and services was justified. Sophistication for this customer base meant solid mathematical foundations, references to key publications, and abilities to teach users about these underpinnings. We succeeded with this for two of the four tools in our *Advisor Series* portfolio of tools.

The problem this created is related to the sophistication of our staff. We hired, in succession, two senior sales executives. They had rich experience bases and great expertise, but they both lacked a deep understanding of what we were selling. Put simply, when your primary clients are Ph.D. electrical engineers and computer scientists, you have to be able to approach them in their comfort zones.

These two senior sales executives expanded our customer base to include companies we would not have imagined buying our software and services, but the new customers could not relate to the key elements of our value proposition. Follow-on sales were limited. We parted ways with these senior sales executives on good terms. We all realized our game was different.

We recruited resellers of our software tools in over twenty countries. Some were very successful, but many were not. All of them leveraged our software tools to sell a modest amount of software and large service projects. Our branded tools gave them competitive advantages in selling services. Their profit margins on the software were respectable but small compared to the service revenues. All of these relationships were eventually not worth the costs of maintaining them.

Another conundrum involved customers requesting ideas, and perhaps proposals, for how to solve problems of importance to them, but then buying the actual solution from other vendors with lower service prices. We gained revenue and profits from our ideas, but it did not seem that these modest returns were sufficient to justify investing scarce talents in such marginal returns.

We explored dramatically reducing prices for our software tools— from $10,000 for a corporate license for twenty copies to a license for $99 per copy. This turned out to be a terrible idea. The cost of the box and manual was much greater than the cost of software. Major corporations purchased one $99 license and then wanted substantial support services, which we already provided—but they wanted these services for free with their $99 purchase.

Understanding market signals is very complicated. You want to provide customers what you are ready to provide but, of course, that is in your interests and not necessarily theirs. The market may have completely unrealistic expectations—for example, the current AI hype cycle—that do not make sense for you or anyone to attempt to serve. Yet, it seems that the market is demanding it.

Addressing this dilemma involves finding the signal in the noise. This can be facilitated by systematically combing the evidence. What evidence? For example, one of the functions of our **Curis Meditor** research portal enables reviewing 50,000 global English-language news articles—per day! Digital assistance helps this process enormously.

This could help you to determine, for instance, that your competitor's announced investment does not make sense and must be a ruse. Thus, there are possibilities for making sense of external market signals. The prospect of internal market assumptions being wrong is a more difficult challenge, as illustrated earlier.

A good starting point is to make these assumptions explicit and then seek evidence that supports or refutes them. Talking to your current and prospective clients and customers is one of the best available means to make such assessments. Perhaps they will eventually convince you of what they really want.

Does society really want a human-centered systems movement? Aggressive pursuit of this idea should be based on extensive market research with a wide range of stakeholder groups. I think the movement needs to emerge rather than simply being announced.

When No One Owns the Problem

There are many problems in our societies, our organizations, and our relationships that no one wants to own. Owning a problem implies a responsibility for solving it. If one recognizes a problem but does not own it, one can often comfortably wait for others to solve it. After all, the problem is not yours.

The most common example of this is the fading market value of your current products and services. Examples include film-based cameras being replaced by digital, photography, inexpensive flip phones by smartphones, and lackluster domestic cars—Mercury, Plymouth, Pontiac, and Oldsmobile—by Asian and European imports. These problems were well recognized, but everybody stuck to the knitting of the status quo.

Another common example is burdensome internal policies and procedures that provide little value and consume significant resources. The worst situations are cultures of compliance laced with administrative incompetence. An interview study we conducted with Department of Defense science and technology executives found that success could be primarily attributed to insanely committed champions who only succeeded by circumventing processes intended to support them.

Another pervasive example is processes intended to enhance a shared value but actually systematically undermine this value. Many of the companies with whom I have worked have well-articulated processes for fostering and managing invention and innovation. However, the prescribed decision-making processes are often circumvented, particularly by senior executives who want their pet ideas supported. Not surprisingly, cynicism quickly emerges and undermines invention and innovation.

All of these examples represent situations where the value of the status quo has significantly eroded. Almost everyone recognizes this, but nobody owns it. Everyone mutually pretends that everything is fine, but also internally acknowledges that things are amuck. What is needed is a leader, at some level, to articulate the problem and advocate a solution.

It is much easier to get everyone to own a well-conceived and broadly recognized solution. This solution represents what we are going to do rather than what we are going to stop doing. It represents the pursuit of success rather than the avoidance of failure. Few people want to accept responsibility for failure. Everyone wants to be recognized for their contributions to success.

The idea of owning a problem suggests some level of blame for the existence of the problem. People try to avoid blame. In contrast, the notion of owning a solution suggests some prospects for success and perhaps recognition for having contributed to this success. People usually aspire to such outcomes.

The lack of ownership of problems is pervasive in the four challenges in this book. Spending the most on health and education while achieving the worst results needs to be owned by the key stakeholders in these domains. The methods and tools I have advocated in this book are intended to enable successful ownership and solutions.

When the Unpopular Position Is Correct

Most organizations and people like to think that everything is under control, proceeding as planned, and the sought outcomes will be realized. If anyone suggests otherwise, they will be chastised for not being team players, perhaps for having bad attitudes, or quite simply for being outright wrong. Unpopular positions are seldom socially acceptable in organizations.

It is worthwhile to understand how these organizational values and norms can result in enormous wastes of resources and time to address problems that desperately need attention if the organization can only accept that they are happening. It is quite common for this recognition to be delayed until no one can deny the organization is in trouble, and resources and time are inadequate for strong, successful responses.

There are few better examples of when we were not paying attention to looming dangers than the Great Recession in 2007–2008 stemming from the bursting of the real estate bubble and the coronavirus pandemic emerging in 2020, chronicled by Michael Lewis in *The Big Short* (2010) and *The Premonition* (2021), respectively. In both cases, political leaders downplayed the risks and magnitudes of the likely consequences.

What most struck me about both events is the extent to which some of the smartest people in the US were betting against the country by shorting investments where severe losses would provide them enormous gains. These people could see what was coming and adjusted their investment strategies accordingly. Most of the population, however, was being misled by their leaders.

Over the past three decades, the US auto industry has grappled with the reality of no longer being market leaders. Chevrolet Impalas and Ford Galaxies have been replaced by Honda Accords and Toyota Camrys as the best-selling cars. Cadillac and Lincoln have been displaced by BMW, Mercedes, and Lexus as aspirational luxury cars. My experiences working with several companies in this industry was that everybody recognized this, but nobody felt empowered to articulate it.

Another challenge emerges when current market positions are not sustainable. In other words, things are not going as well as everybody thinks. In one of my university leadership positions, I discovered that my unit was receiving over 50% of the funds from one division of a government agency. I learned that this was due to a champion in this agency, who was soon to depart. I argued that we needed to diversify. Everyone ignored my arguments until research revenues plummeted.

A value proposition that was once competitive can become no longer competitive. At another university, I met with leaders of an online educational program that I learned was being challenged by a top-ranked competitor that was offering a first-rate program for tuition less than 10% of our offering. I suggested that our moderately-ranked offering would eventually see a greatly reduced market share. Astoundingly, university leaders decided to raise prices. They remain alive but struggle with enrollments.

Technology can undermine market positions. I gave a dinner talk to a large group of insurance executives. I asked each table to discuss what they felt was the greatest threat to their business. A bit later, every table reported the same conclusion—driverless cars. In all US states, premiums are legally limited to matching claims. Many fewer accidents will lead to greatly reduced premiums and, hence, sharply declining revenues.

We worked with these companies to explore alternative scenarios. All scenarios resulted in dramatically decreased revenues over the next 10–15 years as driverless cars gain market share. This led to detailed consideration of the types of insurance needed in this morphed ecosystem. They saw opportunities to compensate in part for the losses. These possibilities made it socially acceptable to discuss the scenarios.

I have consulted with two of the three largest providers of dining services in the US (e.g., via industry, government, and academic cafeterias). It is a fiercely competitive business with very low profit margins. During a strategy offsite, the CEO made a radical proposal to raise prices. The other members of the executive team asserted that this would be the kiss of death.

He outlined the following logic. If prices were raised by $2 per meal, almost all of the increase could go into the quality of the food. He projected that customers would willing to pay for decidedly better meals. They pilot-tested the idea and it was hugely successful and widely deployed. What his team perceived to be a terrible idea was in fact a great idea that resulted in increased revenues and profits.

A competitor, perhaps 2–3 times larger than us, approached me about possibly acquiring us. I had recently been through another acquisition "dance," which we declined, and would have dismissed this opportunity, but considered their CEO a long-term friend. Our company was very carefully managed. My meetings with him and his team suggested that they were not as careful.

This company had developed a computer-based training system, with associated hardware, for training crews of army tanks. They were in the process of bidding on an army contract to build a large number of these training simulators. The CEO was quite confident that they would win. His executive team tried to caution his optimism and not "bet the farm" on winning.

He was not deterred. He was so confident that he made a major investment in constructing the factory to produce the training simulators, before the winner of the competition was decided. They lost to a company that provided a much lower bid. They were left with an empty factory and significantly depleted assets. As far as I know, they never completely recovered from mismanaging these risks.

My experiences across the companies I have founded, and the many who have been clients, is that unpopular positions should be acknowledged and attention invested in due diligence concerning them. I have found that opportunities are very seldom sure things, and you and your team are never as good as you pretend. You can compensate for these shortcomings, in part, by making risk management a core competency. There are rarely, if ever, good opportunities to bet the farm. A portfolio of investments, some larger and many smaller, will lead to at least a few wins and no large losses. Finally, as illustrated by the dining services vignette, an unpopular position may actually be a great opportunity.

When Secondary Issues Dominate

Most organizations have missions and visions for how best to pursue missions, regardless of whether these value statements are formalized or not. Organizational performance metrics indicate how well the organization is performing in terms of revenues, profits, lives saved, or students educated. Successful organizations excel in terms of organizational performance. Most organizations try to improve these metrics.

Peter Drucker famously said, "There is only one purpose of a business: to create a customer." People become customers—or constituencies—of an organization when the organization provides something they value. Understanding, enhancing, and providing value should be the driving issue in an organization. If one does not create a compelling value proposition, organizational success will be limited and likely fleeting.

Are there tradeoffs between organizational performance and other aspects of the organization? For example, might one trade-off organizational performance versus compliance with policies, procedures, and regulations? One certainly would not want the quest for performance to undermine workforce safety or contribute to environmental degradation—although this happens with great regularity.

What about organizational performance versus diversity, equity, and inclusion? My sense is that everyone agrees that a diverse, equitable, and inclusive workforce benefits every type of organization. But how do we get there? At one extreme, we simply stop hiring any white, male candidates. That will quickly get the numbers right. More reasonably, we focus on making sure that female and minority candidates are competitive.

That works too, albeit much more slowly. However, we need to put this in context. I have recently participated in two National Academy workshops on advancement of faculty members (i.e., promotion and tenure). We learned that 90% of faculty members hired nationwide over the past decade have been adjuncts and part-time faculty, with much lower compensation, no benefits, and no job security.

The implications for diversity, equity, and inclusion are that everybody will be treated equally poorly. Unwilling to trim administrative costs, universities will focus on cutting faculty costs and continue to mercilessly exploit everyone with low wages, no benefits, and no job security. My sense is that this was not the intent of the diversity, equity, and inclusion advocates. Should we really try to argue for sustaining the benefits of positions that will steadily disappear?

It seems to me that we need to embrace the future value proposition and the metrics of organizational performance that are sustainable. Are promotion and tenure why a university exists? That is very faculty-centric. Are graduation rates the primary metrics?

That is very student-centric. Another possibility is that universities should prepare graduates to enable innovations that transform society and the economy. Then, of course, we should determine which administrative functions enable such outcomes.

Consider compliance functions. A colleague at Georgia Tech once commented to me that his worst nightmare was a call from the university's Chief Compliance Officer. My experience has been that the worst environment in which to work is a culture of compliance laced with administrative incompetence. The enforcers take everything completely literally.

An experience at Waffle House illustrates this. I had taken two guests from industry to breakfast at the Waffle House around the corner from my office. We ate lightly and the whole bill was around $12. Waffle House does not provide itemized receipts, so the receipt did not indicate what each person had eaten. The university refused to reimburse this expense because I could not prove that no alcohol was consumed. Waffle House does not serve alcohol. I paid the bill personally.

Another university with which I was affiliated decided that faculty and staff had to prove they had actually taken trips for which they reported expenses. They required either a picture of the traveler at the venue visited or a letter from the person visited attesting to the fact that one had actually met with them. This became extremely controversial when a dean refused to ask the Secretary of Defense to provide such a letter. This requirement was eventually rescinded.

I was in a workshop when a senior Air Force executive proclaimed, "I would be comfortable with the government spending $10 to assure that every $1 is appropriately spent." This immediately led to suggestions that the whole government budget be spent on compliance rather than defense, education, or health. The Air Force executive, the most senior person in the workshop, was not amused.

At another university, it was discovered that a faculty member was being reimbursed for travel by the university and another organization—for the same trips. He was reprimanded and his credit card canceled. To be absolutely safe, the university canceled the credit cards of all 6,000 employees. People were now required to use personal credit cards and submit expenses for reimbursement.

To ease this process, the university arranged for one credit card company to issue cards to everyone. The university soon discovered that people were using these cards for personal purchases, for which they did not request reimbursement. This seemed reasonable to many people as the cards were in their names. However, in negotiating with the credit card company, the university had obtained a $10 reduction in the annual fee, which they claimed was effectively income to the employee. Playing it safe, the university again canceled the credit cards of all 6,000 employees.

The university installed a new travel management system so that the filing of travel expenses was automated. The user interface of this system was absolutely terrible, prompting a raft of complaints. At a university-wide meeting where this was addressed, a manager in finance commented that installing this system had enabled reducing staffing by one person. Someone quickly reacted with, "So, now you have 6,000 people spending time doing this job!"

A large aerospace company, with whom I worked, installed an automated timesheet system. Every ten minutes, it prompted each of many thousands of employees to enter the charge code for what they had worked on for the past ten minutes. I asked colleagues how they felt about this. One reaction was, "It's irritating as hell, but you sort of get used to it."

All of these examples illustrate how people adapt to and cope with organizations' proclivities to formulate and implement policies, procedures, and regulations that slowly but surely undermine organizational performance. This is in part due to people wasting time on non-value-added activities. It is also due to the employee cynicism that emerges and festers. The primary purpose of the organization slowly fades into the background.

The challenges I have addressed in this book are plagued by these types of problems. The extreme fragmentation of these ecosystems in the US exacerbates these difficulties. Well-supported information sharing and service coordination can mitigate these difficulties, as demonstrated by Estonia.

When the Organization Is in the Way

There are times when organizations are performing excellently but, despite their confidence, their futures are not bright. Kodak and Polaroid dominated the film and instant photography industries, respectively. My mother inherited a quantity of Kodak stock in the 1930s. It provided generous returns for several decades. People would always seek "Kodak moments" and needed a stock of film. Wouldn't they? Well, no.

These companies knew that digital photography would eventually prevail. Indeed, they invested in R&D that created the technologies that could displace film, instant or otherwise. However, despite their dominance in their markets, they just couldn't "pull the trigger" and cannibalize their existing cash flows. Instead, they let competitors do this, catalyzing their eventual demise.

Why? Their organizations were totally focused on selling film. The metrics in their incentive and reward systems were driven by film sales and decreasing costs of production. They, in effect, provided free cameras to sell film, as Gillette provided free razors to sell blades. What if consumers wanted pictures, but not prints? This future was easy to imagine but difficult to accept if your paycheck depended on prints.

What happened to Digital and Xerox? Digital dominated the minicomputer market and Xerox basically invented personal computing. I worked extensively with Digital, less so but significantly with Xerox. I used the fiftieth PDP-8, of 300,000 sold, to conduct my Ph.D. research at MIT. Digital "owned" the academic research market. The DEC System 10 was next, followed by the VAX series, selling 400,000 units.

The rapid rise of the microcomputer, or personal computer, in the late 1980s, and especially the introduction of powerful 32-bit systems in the 1990s, quickly eroded the value of DEC's systems. DEC's last major attempt to find a space in the rapidly changing market was the 64-bit Alpha. DEC saw the Alpha as a way to re-implement their VAX series, but also employed it in a range of high-performance workstations. The Alpha processor family, for most of its lifetime, was the fastest processor family on the market. However, high Alpha prices could not compete with lower-priced ×86 chips from Intel and AMD.

I was heavily involved with DEC in the 1990s helping them plan several new generations of Alpha chips using our product planning toolkit. One strongly stated objective for each generation was that it retains its **Guinness Book of Records** status as the fastest processor in the world. This objective dominated even when processing speed provided users with minimal benefits. Technical excellence was highly valued in DEC. There was a sense that DEC knew what people needed even if they did not.

The Apple II arrived in 1977, followed by the PC in 1981, and the Apple MAC in 1984 with its classic Super Bowl ad. Many of the appealing features of the MAC were pirated from Xerox. The document company, Xerox, was still trying to figure out how personal computing would sell more paper. Between this perspective and unacceptable market pricing, Xerox fumbled the future.

Back at Digital, CEO Ken Olsen discounted the possibility that anyone would want their own computer. Their DEC Rainbow was clearly too little, too late. IBM, in contrast, realized the era of developing everything yourself was over and outsourced most everything to strategic suppliers (e.g., Microsoft). This was too much of a leap for DEC, presaging their disappearance in 1998.

This brings us to communications and cellphones. I worked extensively with Motorola throughout the 1990s. Their analog technology dominated the market. They had invested in digital technology and knew this was the future, but they did not want to cannibalize their analog market position. Other players, such as Nokia and Qualcomm, did not hesitate. Their digital phones decimated Motorola's market leadership.

Motorola was still innovating, however. A great example is an R&D investment by Motorola in magnetoresistive random access memory, where data is not stored as electric charge, but by magnetic storage. The research team developing this technology was requesting $20 million. Our technology investment analysis tools indicated that the net value was $546 million. After carefully listening to a presentation on the basis of this estimate, the Motorola CEO was sufficiently impressed to commit $40 million with the request that the additional funds be used to reduce risk and accelerate transitioning this technology into their semiconductor business.

The success of this technology contributed to the formation of Freescale Semiconductor, Inc., which was spun off from Motorola in 2004. In 2015, NXP Semiconductors completed its acquisition of Freescale for about $11.8 billion in cash and stock. Including the assumption of Freescale's debt, the purchase price was about $16.7 billion. Despite such successes, Motorola's core communications business was struggling and was sold to Google in 2012 for $12.5 billion, less than the value generated by one significant R&D investment.

Nokia focused on increasingly inexpensive phones and came to dominate the global market. They could not imagine that their $50 phones could be displaced by Apple's $500 iPhone. They were wrong. Consumers did not realize it, but they wanted versatile digital devices that also included a phone. Nokia faded and was sold to Microsoft for $7.2 billion. Microsoft did not fare much better.

Both Motorola and Nokia suffered from being hardware companies that also provided software. Their technical expertise in hardware was superb. However, they tended to develop new operating systems for each generation of devices, which was both expensive and slow. In contrast, Apple's OS and Samsung's Android, courtesy of Google, provided regular updates to all users, including those using past generations of phones. The cultures of Motorola and Nokia, as well as Digital, never embraced this approach.

How does the organization get in the way of change? For all of these cases, organizations had well-developed processes and metrics, which everyone had learned and came to excel in their execution, resulting in bonuses, promotions, and other accolades. These practices had become embedded in their organizational cultures. Everyone "knew" how to act and how to succeed.

However, key elements of this organizational system were premised on assumptions that were no longer true. Many people recognized this. However, it was not socially acceptable to articulate these perceptions. People felt that they needed to maintain focus on keeping the predominant business model functioning and producing. That's what they did until this no longer worked.

All six of these companies were founded with excellent core technology competencies and compelling value propositions. They each led their markets at some point, in some cases for many years. The designs of their organizations, indeed their organizational values and norms, were driven by how they achieved this success. Over time, their markets evolved, typically driven by competitors' offerings. These companies did not evolve in step with their markets. Their value propositions become obsolete.

Joseph Schumpeter (1942) has termed this process "creative destruction." New value propositions are embraced by markets and incumbent competitors fade. This is great for consumers and the economy. However, as these examples illustrate, creative destruction is terrible for the incumbents that cannot adapt. Consequently, the average number of years a successful company remains in the Fortune 500 continually decreases—from over sixty years in the 1950s to less than twenty years today.

The health, education, and energy ecosystems are facing creative destruction. The positive deviants will supplant those stewarding the status quo. These innovators will enable achieving the aspirations in Table 4.1. This could be done more effectively and efficiently, as articulated in Chapters 5–7. However, this requires that "business as usual" not prevail.

When Personalities Trump Competence

Donald Trump is, of course, the ultimate example of this phenomenon. He is a narcissistic psychopath exhibiting extreme forms of grandiosity, exploitative behavior, and a lack of empathy. Fortunately, this severe personality disorder is not common. There are many lessor disorders with which we must deal.

One is fervent optimism. We have all had colleagues who are always upbeat and sure that everything will work out. They are sure that the best outcomes will happen. The archetype of this personality is Sonny, manager of the ***Best Exotic Marigold Hotel***. One of his favorite sayings is, "Everything will be all right in the end and if it is not, then it's not yet the end."

There is also fervent pessimism. My mother, imbued with a "depression mentality"—learned from the Great Depression, 1938 Hurricane, and World War II—often concluded, "If anything can go wrong, it will." I have colleagues who believe and anxiously await all the terrible things that will happen. One colleague pays particular attention to all the things that can go wrong. His insights are often quite useful.

Another category is arrogance involving people who know everything. Their way is always the right way. They are the only ones who understand the central issues. Any potentially good ideas encounter retorts that "we already did that." The worst case involves people who know absolutely how everything in life is going wrong. Such folks are not interested in your perspectives.

A special category of arrogance includes people who are combative. They know that you are wrong. They know the right way to do things. Further, they are sure that you don't know what you are doing. They are dismissive of you and everybody else. They are not really sure why you or anybody else ventures to offer opinions or suggestions.

Then there is the category of the oppressed. Their lives are laced with woe. The organization, indeed the world, provides them no support. They have to struggle to accomplish everything by themselves. An extreme of this category are those whose lives are a mess. Relationships, children, and even their homes conspire against them. They feel compelled to relate these woes to everyone.

How can one best cope with the above types of personalities? A strategy of listening but not reacting might work unless you are the leader of the team. Then, you have to facilitate the interactions between the troublesome team members and everybody else. You cannot let these unfortunate behaviors undermine the team and possibly the whole organization.

This can be rather problematic when the people exhibiting these behaviors are among the highest performers on the team. You do not want to get rid of them because they are really good at what they do. You might try to convert those in the troublesome categories to become optimists. This will likely require some one-on-one mentoring. This special attention can provide opportunities to acknowledge these team members' skills and contributions, while asking them to change their approaches to others.

Leading a team involves much more than simply getting everyone to do their job well. Excellent taskwork is necessary for success, but not sufficient. You also need excellent teamwork. Sometimes this requires mentoring excellent task workers to become better team workers. This may involve mentoring some types of personalities to overcome their natural tendencies. Everyone on the team will appreciate this.

Such abilities are central to the possibilities for the human-centered systems movement. You need to get all your talent rowing in the same direction. This may require more attention than you expect. There are risks that personalities can become major distractions. However, with attention and care, you can foster the synergies you need.

When Abilities to Execute Are Secondary

It's a great idea, but can we do it? Can we make it happen? We are going to boil the oceans and then provide everybody with gourmet seafood dinners. Okay for those who eat seafood, but how is this going to be accomplished? Making the elements of a solution happen—executing—tends to be an enormous challenge.

What if everyone in the world had smartphones, state-of-the-art laptops, and high-performance broadband connectivity? Wouldn't everything be okay then, at least eventually? These capabilities would help, but life involves much more than technology. What about economic opportunities and access to food, healthcare, and education?

I have been involved in seemingly endless conversations about digitally transforming an enterprise. The idea is to eliminate paper, become totally data-driven, and embrace evidence-based decision-making. Sounds great if data are available and curated. Let's reflect on what success will require.

If one wants data-driven, evidence-based strategy discussions, there are a few precursors:

- Does one have the requisite data over a meaningful period of time?
- Have these datasets been curated to ensure that they represent a valid corpus?
- Have inconsistencies and incompatibilities across datasets been identified?
- Have models been identified that can provide valid projections of future outcomes?

Assuring appropriate answers to these questions is difficult work. In my experience, many organizations treat these questions much too lightly. They want to avoid the difficult work and "install" solutions quickly. Two examples provide good illustrations.

A large aerospace company asked me to help them determine what knowledge management solution to acquire. I asked them, "Where is poor knowledge management hurting you?" After much discussion, they chose foreign military sales. We then proceeded to address that one specific problem to learn what knowledge management really meant and how it could help them.

The CEO of a large appliance company asked me what knowledge management solution they should acquire. I asked him the same leading question. His team concluded that production plans often resulted in appliances being produced that no one had ordered and appliances not being produced that Walmart, in particular, had ordered. They noted Walmart because this customer charged a penalty for undelivered products (i.e., the profit they would have made had the products been delivered).

We tracked down how production forecasts were developed. Field representatives provided projections of appliance sales, by product, in their region. These forecasts were compiled and resulted in production plans. We talked with field representatives about how they came up with their forecasts. A common answer was, "I look at last quarter's orders and decide where to increment them up or down. By the way, what do you do with those numbers?"

The knowledge management problem was that key participants in the production planning process did not know how their inputs affected the process. Beyond managing knowledge, the company needed to do a much better job at sharing it. This led the company to create an initiative focused on who needs to know what and how this knowledge is shared.

Once one gets past the above hurdles of data access, curation, and modeling, several new questions become central:

- What economic, social, and political forces are likely to affect the future?
- How are these forces likely to impact our projections of future revenues?
- Are our competencies well positioned for this competition?
- Where will we experience challenges—performance, cost, and customer satisfaction?

To address these types of questions, we need to move beyond "what is" to address "what if." Questions associated with "what is" can be addressed with the datasets noted above. These datasets are inherently about what has happened, not what will or might happen.

"What if" questions can be informed by but not answered by empirical data. This is simply because the future has not yet happened. Nevertheless, execution happens in the future. A digital strategy, or equivalent, that is limited to examining the past will be very much inadequate. Emerging forces, their impacts, and their abilities to compete are all about executing in the future, a future that is quite likely to be significantly different from the past.

Abilities to execute are usually addressed within the context of the incumbent enterprise's abilities to scale what it has long been doing. This perspective has merits—unfortunately, often only briefly. A company's ability to steadily increase quality and decrease costs can sustain and perhaps grow revenues for existing offerings. This worked for Henry Ford's Model T for almost twenty years, but the competition came to offer better models in more than one color.

How can an organization catch up with what will be needed? How should they plan to execute in the future? These questions tend to be major challenges, often insurmountable challenges. Many, perhaps most, organizations think they are doing their best to execute their processes today. Their processes may be outmoded and inefficient, but they have little time to think about this possibility.

Consider briefly the domains of healthcare, education, and energy. Technologies will potentially impact all three domains. Telehealth and artificial intelligence will change key elements of healthcare. Online learning, including the unbundling of learning, will profoundly affect the economics of post-secondary education. Renewable, yet intermittent, energy sources will challenge the reliable and resilient provision of energy.

These three domains are likely to execute in the future much differently than they execute today. Those who wait to see what happens are unlikely to be tomorrow's leaders. In contrast, those who see execution in the future as primary, and consequently play central roles in designing these futures, will undoubtedly lead their domains into those futures.

Several years ago, I was engaged with a large information technology company in developing an R&D strategic plan. They had an agreed-upon social norm that surprised me. Apparently, marketing had a tendency to dream up wild ideas. Engineering and manufacturing would explain the difficulties of executing their visions. Someone from marketing would invariably say, "Oh, come on. How difficult could that really be?" The technical folks complained to top management. This execution-oriented challenge was henceforth banned.

When Stakeholders Thwart Change

People who are advantaged by the status quo tend to be averse to changing it. Consequently, those who are favored in this way tend to herald its merits and disdain the alternatives. Why wouldn't we continue the policies and strategies that generously rewarded them in the past? As a leader of an organization needing to entertain fundamental change, you need to be able to understand and manage such reluctance.

I served on an Air Force Scientific Advisory Board study of science and technology investment strategies. We considered what investments were needed to assure "pervasive battlespace awareness." I commented that this could be enabled in many ways, but key stakeholders on the study committee reminded me that they produce satellites, airplanes, and missiles. They needed those solutions to prevail.

This reflects their strong desire to sustain investments in incumbent capabilities and sustain current jobs. Not surprisingly, this motivation is pervasive. People do not want their economic supply chain to be disrupted. They want paychecks, promotions, and pensions to flow as they expected. They want this economic supply chain to persist perpetually. Of course, that has really never been the case.

Despite easy automation of routine clerical jobs, manual labor is retained to keep people employed. I encountered this when living in Europe. Despite strong priorities and desires to sustain investments in incumbent capabilities, these positions were steadily disappearing. It appeared that a primary motivation for sticking to the status quo was the desire to avoid the costs of training people for new jobs.

Moving to professional personnel, there is no reason for each faculty member to prepare fresh class notes for each course. Nevertheless, this time-consuming rite of passage continues. Every faculty member gets to research and determine how best to teach western civilization, a topic taught for well over 1,000 years. How many new ways can there be to do this?

Disciplines that dominate academic cultures tend to be sustained despite their seeming marginal relevance. For example, in my world, many faculty members extoll the virtues of mathematics, even when purely mathematical solutions to the real problems at hand are intractable. Faculty members who pursue empirical approaches to these problems are disdained as applied practitioners—not pursuing fundamental knowledge.

The concern among these recalcitrant stakeholders is not employment. It is self-esteem. They have spent decades becoming highly skilled and expert at what they, and their colleagues, perceive to be fundamental and pervasively important skills. The possibility that these skills, while still important, are now of limited rather than pervasive value is very difficult for them to accept. Thus, they do their best to thwart change.

Fortunately, as Max Planck asserted, disciplines advance by funerals. Thus, faculty members who strongly defend yesterday's status quo eventually disappear, while making as much fuss as they can in the process. Stakeholders thwarting change are recurring phenomena and a challenge for leaders trying to balance faculty interests. However, time heals the challenges at hand with, of course, younger stakeholders, perhaps unconsciously, awaiting their turn.

A common refrain is, "We've always done it this way." Thus, for example, GM's executives insist that the first year of a new car has to be a coupe, despite the fact that the public is only buying sedans and now, of course, SUVs. GM eventually abandoned this practice after dramatically losing market share. Executives thwarted change as long as they could.

Another example is college's expectations of student attrition. Within engineering, the common guidance was, "Look to your left and look to your right. Next year only one of the three of you will still be here." Why is this long-held norm a good idea? Why were "weed out" courses created? Fortunately, student success initiatives have significantly eroded this tradition.

Underlying all of the above is a strong tendency to revere "the good old days," even though they were not really good for everybody—or even anybody. Before cars, New York City had to remove 100,000 tons of horse manure each year. No one missed it. Few people want to get rid of electricity, refrigeration, air conditioning, and indoor plumbing. The good old days were more old than good.

How about values and norms such as honesty, discipline, and hard work, possibly pulling oneself up by one's bootstraps? Such values and norms tend to only make sense for those stakeholders with requisite opportunities. These are often the stakeholders with the economic resources to be healthy, get educated, and pursue opportunities. Others may be able to relate to these aspirations but be in no position to pursue them.

Beyond concerns about losses of jobs, income, benefits, and self-esteem, there is another primary reason to thwart change. Key stakeholders may not trust change in the sense of being wary that their interests will be discounted and ignored. Their experiences tell them that no one will protect them from the downside of change. History provides much evidence that they are correct. The winners relish their victories and disdain the losers, even though losing was built into the game for many people.

Several years ago, I studied how defense companies succeeded in transitioning from defense to commercial markets. I could only find one company that transitioned successfully while retaining the majority of the same employees—Kaman Corporation. It is much more common for companies to redeploy financial and physical assets without retaining the previously valuable people and competencies.

In another engagement, I helped a large defense electronics company consider a transition to commercial electronics. The most outspoken opponents were the engineers who believed they worked on the cutting edge of technology in defense and would be relegated to mundane applications in commercial markets. The company decided to abandon these commercial aspirations.

I had a similar experience with the transition from my first to second companies. We had long felt that we needed product lines that provided recurring revenue beyond our service revenues for research and design services. In developing a portfolio of products, we learned that customers wanted the tools hosted on IBM PCs, or maybe Apple Macs. Our software staff had complete disdain for these platforms compared to the $100,000 engineering workstation to which they were accustomed.

Consequently, the launch of the second company included only one of the twenty-plus software engineers of the first company, as well as one person in finance and one in marketing. We had to consciously build a new culture around low-end workstations, an 800 number for customer support, and other functions customers expected. Also of great importance were product upgrades every twelve months or less.

Can everybody win from transformational change? You need well-articulated plans for those who want to be part of the transformation, including new roles, objectives, and incentives, as well as the training required to succeed. However, you should not expect everyone to join the process. Many—hopefully not most—of your best people will have other opportunities and priorities. For some, their self-images (e.g., as mathematicians or software engineers) will not be compatible with where you are headed.

You can expect that significant stakeholders will attempt to thwart your aspirations for fundamental change. Their reasons may be quite rational, far from capricious. This will be less of a problem if you understand and expect such reactions. Your primary objective is to lead the organization forward to sustainable success. Your job is **not** to make sure everybody is happy.

The applicability of these insights to how we address the four challenges in this book is rather obvious. Despite the appealing projections of greatly improved services and attractive economic outcomes, the stewards of the status quo will be uncomfortable. Their positions, incomes, and benefits will be challenged. How can you convince them to support the transformation?

When Leadership Makes a Difference

Exemplary leaders face difficult circumstances, work with others to devise plans for addressing these circumstances, cultivate support for these plans, and execute plans with a degree of success. Such success in difficult circumstances is possible. However, as the following vignettes illustrate, leadership is crucial. If top leaders remain stewards of the status quo, fundamental change will not happen. Leadership is the most important competency augmented by vision, strategy, communications, and collaboration.

National leaders are among the most obvious exemplars. Abraham Lincoln and the Civil War (1861–1865), as chronicled in *Team of Rivals* (Goodwin, 2006), showcased his abilities as a shrewd navigator of people and positions to achieve enormous, albeit painful, success. Teddy Roosevelt and the Progressive Era (1901–1909), chronicled in *The Bully Pulpit* (Goodwin, 2013), illustrated commitments to basic principles rather than the power brokers.

Franklin Roosevelt and the New Deal (1933–1945), combined with Winston Churchill and World War II (1940–1945), are wonderfully portrayed in *Fateful Choices* (Kershaw, 2007). They needed to negotiate feasible and viable decisions to address and counter decisions by Hitler, Mussolini, Stalin, and Tojo. These two leaders needed to understand their respective constituencies and how they could engender support for a cataclysmic confrontation. They succeeded.

Corporate leaders might include Carnegie, Morgan, Rockefeller, and Vanderbilt, but amassing monopolistic power does not seem to me to epitomize leadership as much as simply the accumulation of raw market power. Instead, consider Louis Gerstner and IBM (1993–2002), Bill Gates and Microsoft (1975–2000), and Steve Jobs and Apple (1976–2011). These leaders transformed their enterprises.

IBM had its highest share price in 1990, but was on the path to losing billions in 1993. Louis Gerstner, the new IBM CEO, is widely credited with transforming IBM. Gerstner joined IBM in April 1993. During his tenure, the company's share price increased by more than 800%, and its market value grew by $180 billion. The company also gained market share in key strategic areas, including servers, software, storage, and microelectronics.

Microsoft at first dismissed the Internet and Netscape's web browser, introduced in 1994. By May of 1995, however, Microsoft CEO Bill Gates had thrown his company wholeheartedly into joining the "Internet tidal wave." They released Internet Explorer as an add-on for Windows 95. More recently, Microsoft introduced Azure cloud computing services in 2010 and now is second in market share behind Amazon Web Services.

Apple was on the brink of fizzling out, struggling to find a consistently profitable source of revenue. Instead of continuing to aimlessly pursue marginal product ideas, Apple, with Steve Jobs again leading, began to focus once more on creating beautiful consumer electronics, starting with the iMac in 1998. The iPod was an even bigger success, selling over 100 million units within six years of its 2001 launch. The iPhone, another smash hit, was released in 2007 and resulted in enormous year-over-year increases in sales. The iPad followed in 2010. Apple changed its name in 2007 from Apple Computer to just Apple.

Academia has been led by many transformational leaders. Charles Eliot, President of Harvard (1869–1909) transformed this provincial college into a pre-eminent American research university. Karl Compton, President of MIT (1930–1948) and highly involved in supporting World War II efforts, transformed MIT to become a national research asset. The federal funds that subsequently flowed to MIT have been immense. More recently, Charles Vest, President at MIT (1990–2004) and the National Academy of Engineering (2007–2013), spearheaded expansions into the fields of brain and cognitive sciences, nanotechnology, genomic medicine, biological engineering, and engineering systems.

Wayne Clough, President at Georgia Tech (1994–2008), oversaw $1 billion in new construction, increased retention, and graduation rates, achieved a higher nationwide ranking and pursued a much larger student body, including programs that encouraged undergraduate research, offered international experiences, and made college more affordable for low-income students. Clough went on to become Secretary of the Smithsonian Institution (2008–2014). His Provost, Jean-Lou Chameau became President of Cal Tech (2006–2013).

The above listing only includes men, mainly because political, industrial, and academic organizations were almost always led by white men. Women found other paths to leadership. Clara Barton founded the American Red Cross in 1881. Margaret Sanger opened the first birth control clinic in the United States in 1916, which evolved into the Planned Parenthood Federation.

The early twentieth century was an innovative period for cosmetics. Elizabeth Arden founded her cosmetics empire, Elizabeth Arden, Inc., in 1910. Helena Rubinstein founded Helena Rubinstein, Inc. cosmetics company in 1915. Both women became among the richest women in the world.

Madam C.J. Walker made her fortune by developing and marketing a line of cosmetics and hair care products for black women through the Madam C.J. Walker Manufacturing Company, founded in 1910. She is recognized as the first female self-made millionaire in America.

Women comprised almost 60% of US college students in 2020. Almost 51% of students in medical schools and more than 52% of the students in law schools were women. Women comprise 27% of the Members of Congress. Roughly 70% are Democrats. Much of the growth in female Members has emerged since the 1990s. There is a steadily growing number, now over forty, of female CEOs among the Fortune 500. These trends portend increasing numbers of women in leadership positions.

Leadership is not just a matter of being in charge, which can be characterized as management or perhaps administration. Exemplary leaders face difficult circumstances, work with others to devise plans for addressing these circumstances, cultivate support for these plans, and execute plans with a degree of success. Management or administration are seldom adequate in such situations. Leadership is the most important competency augmented by vision, strategy, communications, and collaboration.

Leadership will be a critical ingredient in pursuit of the vision outlined in this book. The execution and success of the human-centered systems movement will require many leaders in multiple domains, communicating, and coordinating, sharing lessons learned, and celebrating early, albeit modest, wins in the process of transforming vision to reality.

Conclusions

The discussions and guidance in this chapter are applicable to a wide range of issues in organizational life. This should not be a surprise. Moving beyond quick fixes is a perennial and pervasive challenge.

I have used numerous vignettes of experiences in a broad range of domains, not limited to health, education, and energy. I have learned that compelling examples can come from a range of sources. The essential challenges of strategic management are ubiquitous.

The organizational challenges I have outlined and illustrated in this chapter represent fundamental hurdles that must be surmounted to enable the fundamental changes I have envisioned in this book. The success of the human-centered systems movement will depend on successful organizational and individual change.

References

Goodwin, D.K. (2006). *Team of Rivals: The Political Genius of Abraham Lincoln*. New York: Simon & Schuster.

Goodwin, D.K. (2013). *The Bully Pulpit: Theodore Roosevelt, William Howard Taft, and the Golden Age of Journalism*. New York: Simon & Schuster.

Hanawalt, E.S., & Rouse, W.B. (2010). Car wars: Factors underlying the success or failure of new car programs. *Journal of Systems Engineering*, 13 (4), 389–404.

Kershaw, I. (2007). *Fateful Choices: Ten Decisions That Changed the World, 1940–1941*. New York: Harper.

Liu, C., Rouse, W.B., & Yu, Z. (2015). When transformation fails: Twelve case studies in the American automobile industry. *Journal of Enterprise Transformation*, 5 (2), 71–112.

Schumpeter, J. (1942). *Capitalism, Socialism, and Democracy*. New York: Harper & Row.

Index